**THE BUSINESS ENVIRONMENT
OF THE SEVENTIES**

Special Report to Management

THE BUSINESS ENVIRONMENT OF THE SEVENTIES

A Trend Analysis for Business Planning

EARL B. DUNCKEL

WILLIAM K. REED

IAN H. WILSON

General Electric Company

McGRAW-HILL BOOK COMPANY
New York   St. Louis   San Francisco   Dusseldorf   London
Mexico   Panama   Sydney   Toronto

Library of Congress Catalog Card Number 70-127968
07-018207-8

234567890 HDBP 754321

PREFACE

We have developed this book in the belief that business planning urgently requires a new dimension — socio-political forecasting — and with the hope that our message may help to catalyze corporate action on this front.

In an age in which "everything relates to everything else," it no longer makes sense for business to ignore the serious impact of social and political developments on its operations. Business managers may recognize this, intellectually — or in retrospect: but in practice regrettably little attention is given to trying to anticipate these trends, to helping shape their course and to factoring their implications into business planning.

The purpose of this book, therefore, is not to foreclose new thinking about the future by presenting a supposedly definitive view of the next decade, but rather to stimulate further thought and action. Indeed, if we were to create an aura of inevitability about these

v

forecasts, we would be undermining our own philosophy that the future cries out for present action and there remains considerable latitude for individual and corporate initiatives.

It is important, too, to stress that these forecasts are not ours or those of General Electric Company. They represent a view of the future as seen through the eyes of some of this country's leading authorities in a wide variety of disciplines and occupations. The synthesis is ours; but the basic ideas are theirs.

I would like to record here our deep appreciation for the time and effort spent by all those who shared their ideas so generously with us (their names are listed in Appendix A). Without their willing participation we could not have progressed so far with our beginning program of research and analysis. I should also like to thank the many people in General Electric who gave us much needed assistance in reviewing and reporting on the literature and in interviewing distinguished thought leaders in their communities.

Most particularly, although the three authors of this book share the responsibility for the research and conclusions, Earl B. Dunckel and I owe a special debt to Ian H. Wilson, who took the leadership in synthesizing our findings into a useable form and reporting them lucidly and comprehensively.

Monitoring the business environment is a continuous task; but it can be a co-operative one. Though the derivation of policy implications must be particularized to each company, the basic data gathering and trend identification can be a joint venture. Indeed, the field is so vast that it would be presumptuous for any one company to believe that it could be constantly alert to all developments. So we share our initial findings willingly and hope that others who may be stimulated to move into this field will also contribute their ideas to the common pool of knowledge and shared experience.

William K. Reed, Manager
Business Environment
General Electric Company

CONTENTS

THE BUSINESS ENVIRONMENT OF THE SEVENTIES

1

PURPOSE AND PERSPECTIVE

> "To complain of the age we live in, to murmur at
> the present possessors of power, to lament the
> past, to conceive extravagant hopes of the future
> are the common dispositions of the greatest part
> of mankind."
> Edmund Burke

Passage through an era of radical change, such as we are likely to experience in the Seventies, produces reactions that vary widely among individuals and institutions. At one extreme are the "extravagant hopes" of those who see in new technology and increasing affluence the promise of economic growth, individual prosperity, increasing leisure and education. At the other pole we find the dismay of those who lament the passing of the old order, the disgust of those who see no place for man in an increasingly mechanistic culture, and the impatience of those who despair at the slow pace of institutional change.

Equally diverse are the attitudes toward the need for, and the feasibility of, long-range planning when future developments are so hard to foresee. There are some who would argue that planning is an exercise in futility when so much is uncertain; that no single institution (not even the Federal government)—still less, an individual — can hope to shape its future; that the best one can hope for is rapid and successful <u>adaptation</u> to the inevitable.

There is, however, a contrary view which espouses a more activist philosophy. It finds its expression in a conviction that we can, in some sense, impose our own direction on the course of change. In this view, change is seen quite as much as an opportunity, presenting options and possibilities, as a problem. Sometimes known as "causative anticipation," this philosophy holds that it is possible to conceive of a desired goal; to work backwards from this goal through the necessary stages for achieving it; and then to set in motion a course of action that will lead from the present toward the desired future. This is not to say, of course, that total control of the future is attainable: the limits of the possible have, of course, to be recognized in any situation. Yet the range of choice is wide, and the possibilities for action are numerous.

To see the wide disparity between the end results of action and inaction, we need only speculate on the possible courses of two major developments in our society — the urban minority problem and environmental pollution. It is not hard to see that, left to run their course, with no attempt being made at corrective action, both problems could have well-nigh catastrophic consequences. In the one case, our society would be polarized into warring camps, with the white suburban majority attempting to repress a rebellious urban minority. In the other, we would be choked with our own garbage, suffocated by a smog-laden atmosphere, poisoned by polluted water, deafened by the cacophony of our urban living.

Yet in each case we can conceive of an alternative future. We can, for instance, envisage the possibility of a more open equitable society in which there is true equality of opportunity and a more liveable environment in which the human dimension is dominant. The differences from the first conceptions would be startling. But these futures can only be realized by decisive and determined action. To achieve the first results we have only to let events take their course, to ensure that "things are in the saddle and ride mankind," and to react to each new disaster with makeshift programs. To achieve the second, we must first define our goals in fairly precise terms so that the needed programs of action can be identified. Then we must summon

2

up the will and perseverance to initiate and complete the action.

Absolutely fundamental to such an activist philosophy is a new way of looking at the future. We can no longer be satisfied with viewing it as merely "interesting" (as a fortune teller's fantasy), or as pre-ordained, or as an intellectual exercise in speculation. It is, rather, to be seen as a major determinant of present action. The new art of "futurism," embracing the methods and knowledge of many disciplines and utilizing the techniques of systems planning and cost-effectiveness analysis, comes on the scene at a time of world-wide flux and uncertainty, when many had begun to fear that we would become the servants rather than the masters of the techno-logical and social changes we had set in motion. This new way of thinking about the future in a systematic way gives real hope that we may be able to make conscious, timely decisions about the direction in which we want to go and that our values may determine the utiliza-tion of our capabilities rather than the other way around.

There can be little doubt that action rather than reaction is the correct course to choose. For business in particular, any other choice would be an implicit admission of failure which would lead to a slow stagnation and a loss of standing and credibility in society. Change, indeed, makes planning more, not less, necessary for busi-ness success. Change also, however, makes planning more diffi-cult and demands that it be more flexible.

This volume is thus dedicated more to the exposition of a concept than to a particular view of the future. Though subsequent chapters are devoted to projections of possible social, political and economic change, they should be considered indicative rather than definitive. The more important consideration is the underlying concept, which can be stated in a pair of propositions:

1. That the "internal environment" of a corporation cannot be viewed in isolation from the "external environment" of which it is a part

2. That there exists a limited, but real, possibility of helping shape the course and character of that external environment, rather than merely reacting to it

THE NEED FOR ENVIRONMENTAL FORECASTING

Part of the management rhetoric of the Sixties had been the asser-
tion that "no business plan is worth the paper it is written on if it
doesn't take into consideration social and political factors." The
principle formulated in this statement is, without question, sound:
but it is one to which most managers have given little more than lip
service. The fact remains that, even today, a great deal of our
forecasting, and most of our planning, is still just a two-dimensional affair involving only economic and technological projections.

The typical corporation now finds itself the focal point for a be-
wildering number of external forces that impact on it from every
angle. The larger the company, the more likely is this to be true,
for the bigger target will be hit more frequently and probably with
greater force. There is virtually no major trend in the social, political and economic arena, at home and abroad, that does not affect
in some way the operations or future growth of the corporation. To
create an "early warning system" on only two fronts — technological
and economic — (Fig. 1) is, therefore, apt to leave a company highly
vulnerable to attack from an unexpected quarter.

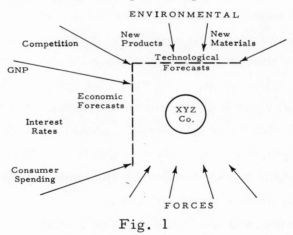

Fig. 1

In this typical situation business planning is based almost exclusively
upon the projections of economic trends (estimates of future Gross
National Product components, disposable income, market segments
and the like) and technological forecasting (for instance, the probable

4

development cycle of new materials, new products, new processes; assessment of competitive research). For the rest, managers have been too ready just to make generalized assessments of the conventional and obvious political factors — war, an election, international monetary problems — or to rely on the caveat, expressed or implied, "other things being equal."

However, if there is one lesson that the disruptions of the past decade should have taught us, it is that "other things" most certainly will not be "equal." To look no further than at the outbursts in our cities and on our campuses in recent years, it should be obvious that social moods, personal attitudes and political action have been dynamic and determinative forces in the United States. To overlook this or to assume away this fact — or even to assert that it affects only other institutions (government, colleges, high schools) — would be an unforgivable and unbusinesslike flight from reality in business planning.

It is not necessary to get into an argument over which set of forces — economic, technological, social or political — is most significant. Indeed, in reporting on our original study (see p. 10), we noted:

> Significantly, the trends identified in this series of dialogues were not primarily scientific and technological in character: they were concerned, rather, with problems of "social perfectability." This does not, of course, mean that science and technology have ceased to contribute to social progress; only that individual, institutional and social attitudes toward, and uses of, these forces may well be more determinative of the course of change. Indeed, this statement will bear the interpretation that science and technology are <u>the</u> basic forces, and that the only questions relate to the ends toward which they should be directed.

The important consideration is to recognize the relevance of all these forces to business planning and to a more complete understanding of probable developments of our society.

It is vital to future business success, therefore, that managers recognize the need for two further dimensions to the planning process — social and political trend analysis (Fig. 2).

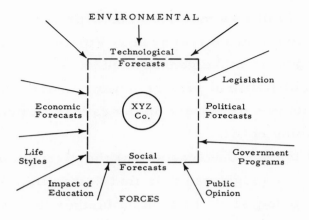

ENVIRONMENTAL

Technological
Forecasts

Legislation

Economic
Forecasts

XYZ
Co.

Political
Forecasts

Life
Styles

Social
Forecasts

Government
Programs

Impact of
Education

FORCES

Public
Opinion

Fig. 2

If this socio-political forecasting is done comprehensively and successfully, on both a short- and long-term basis, a business is not so
likely to be taken by surprise by shifting public moods, changing aspirations of employees or customers and legislative or administrative
action by government. What is still not fully appreciated by most
businesses is that these forces can be quite as devastating in their
impact on profitability as the brilliant shift in market strategy or
product development by a competitor.

When all is said and done, of course, the element of chance or
surprise will always remain in the picture. One certain prediction
is that managers will have to learn how to live with, and manage,
uncertainty: and none of us is ever comfortable in such a situation.
The Seventies will, therefore, be (in that sense) an "uncomfortable,"
challenging decade for business managers, with no latitude for
complacency.

However, within such a four-sided framework — of social, political, economic and technological forecasting — business plans can
then be formulated with greater assurance that all predictable environmental factors have been taken into consideration. With anything less, an otherwise sound strategy for gaining market position
by buying out another company can be thwarted by an antitrust suit;
a plant's labor market can, as it has in several cities, change with
surprising rapidity and prove inadequate for planned production
schedules and methods; or a new piece of legislation or an adminis-

trative action can eliminate a whole market or an important segment of it, as the DDT and cyclamates cases proved in 1969.

To anticipate one of the more significant findings of our study, we can predict that the key problem for business in the next decade will be environmental adjustment and that, increasingly, business will have to develop what one observer has termed "an instinct for survival in a political world." Clearly, however, this "adjustment" and "instinct for survival" must not be merely a process of response and accommodation: it must also embrace the far more demanding task of learning to shape one's environment creatively.

INSTITUTIONALIZING THE FORECASTING PROCESS

If, however, we are to proceed beyond the point of lip service to the need for environmental forecasting, then we must make a commitment of time, attention and resources. We must, in other words, institutionalize the process by taking four essential steps:

- Deciding to make the "four-sided framework" a required part of the planning process;
- Devising, and implementing, a systematic method for monitoring the environment and for "making sense of change" by looking for patterns among the multitudinous pieces of seemingly unrelated trends;
- Making a comprehensive analysis of these trend patterns to derive their full implications for business planning;
- Integrating socio-political forecasts into business plans.

This is not a volume on the methodology of environmental forecasting (on which, in any case, there is more groping than certainty), so the following notes are intended only to indicate the general dimensions of the forecasting process.

The basic determination to broaden the perspectives of business planning is, of course, one that only top management can make, or make effective. If they are unaware of, or unpersuaded by, the importance of socio-political forecasting, then business planning will remain essentially a two-dimensional affair. This is not to say that planning specialists should be cast in a merely passive role in this

7

regard. The burden of proof is on them, after all, to demonstrate the feasibility of this type of forecasting and its specific relevance to their company's business needs. However, it is only top management that can require this forecasting to be a part of the planning process; that can assign responsibility and resources for this work; and that can probe to ensure the environmental soundness of any plan that is to be reviewed and approved. The whole complex process must start by the simple top-level injunction, "Let it be done!"

The second need — for systematic monitoring of the environment — can, of course, be met in many ways. The following section describes briefly one approach taken by General Electric, but Olaf Helmer's Delphi Method, Herman Kahn's scenarios and many other approaches are at least equally valid in mapping out what is presumed to be the "most probable" future. Whatever approach is chosen, however, cannot be undertaken on a "one shot" basis: continuity of monitoring is absolutely essential if the early warning system is to operate effectively. Continuity and in-depth analysis of specific developments are needed to ensure the full relevance and comprehension of study findings. And, since there is a limit to the comprehensiveness of even the most sophisticated system, we should try to identify the most probable discontinuities, or breaks in trend-lines, to which our monitoring should give priority. If we cannot monitor all fronts at all times, then we must concentrate on the most critical points. For, clearly, it is the sudden departure from a projection of past trends — the break point from which trends develop in a new direction — that would disrupt our planning more than will even quite major deviations between forecasting and events along the same trend line.

The third stage may prove to be the most difficult of all: bringing the generalized forecast down to specific implications for each particular business, function, role. We are all most apt to be blind in matters that closely affect us, as one episode connected with our first study demonstrates. This report contained a significant volume of comment on such matters as the growing impatience of youth, its rejection of authoritarianism, its concern over the Vietnam war and the racial issue. Many of the educators we talked with in our study recognized these and other developing trends — recognized, too, the university's traditional resistance to change — but failed to perceive the full consequences for the campus. (Up to that point Berkeley had been the only instance of major disruption.) In retrospect, we can see that all the ingredients for a campus riot were present — and, in large part, identified in our study; but the specific incident of a student riot was not projected by any of the educators. Similarly, it would seem that many business managers have been largely blind to the consequences — in new life styles, work aspirations, attitudes to social problems — of the very affluence that business has generated.

Yet, however difficult the exercise may be, we must each make a thoroughgoing and conscientious effort to answer, in fairly precise terms, the question "What does this trend mean for me? For my work? For my business?" Even in a relatively small company, the number and variety of business implications to be derived from environmental forecasting is such that this work cannot be done exclusively by the forecasting component. This component must indeed suggest broad areas for investigation and catalyze the questioning process in other components, but the most valuable answers are likely to be those that are reached by those who are closest to the point of impact of environmental forces.

Then, and only then, will it be possible to move to the fourth phase — integrating the socio-political forecasts into the business plan. There are many difficulties along this path, one being that of relating the "soft" data derived from socio-political analysis to the relatively "hard" data of economic and technological forecasting. One possible way to bridge this gap is to reduce both sets of data to their basic assumptions and then to examine the two sets of assumptions for consistency. Another way would be to develop a business plan, as at present, on the basis of economic and technological inputs, and then to determine whether the social and political projections tend to confirm or deny the feasibility of this plan. A third, and perhaps preferable, approach would be to deduce from the various data four sets of parameters (opportunities and constraints) within which the business plan must be evolved.

These few notes do no more than highlight a few of the problems, and possible solutions, in the way of environmental forecasting. It is to be hoped, however, that neither the novelty of the work nor the "sponginess" of the data will deter managers from a most necessary task — a task that entails a whole new way of looking at a business in its total societal context.

THE GENERAL ELECTRIC STUDY

The major part of this book is devoted to reporting the principal findings of a continuous environmental monitoring system established in General Electric in 1967. The system has operated so far for two years (through the fall of 1969) and proceeded through three stages:

1. An initial study, which sketched in the main features of the future business environment. This study can be likened to a single 360° sweep of the early warning system radar revealing a number of still poorly defined "blips" on the screen.

2. The first in a series of more detailed studies to define, with greater precision, the nature, trajectory and probable impact of the forces represented by these "blips." This first in-depth analysis was devoted to the minority environment of the Seventies, following the logic of the initial study which identified the urban/minority problem as "the dominant one on the domestic social, political and economic scene for the next ten years."

3. A continuing re-evaluation of the initial study in the light of new thinking and studies, measured against the actual course of developing events (the continuing general monitoring of the impending environment).

The focus of this monitoring has been on the next five to ten years with the 1975-1980 period as the outer range of predictions. In the main, too, it deals with developments during this period in the United States. This is not to say that a world view, particularly at a time of increasing internationalization of business, is unimportant; but some limitations had to be placed on the study to keep it manageable. A brief chapter on assumptions concerning world-wide developments is included merely to provide the "international context" in which domestic events may well be taking place.

As an experimental effort to provide a framework for future planning, these studies attempted to take a broad survey of the major trends and forces re-shaping American society, as seen through the eyes of some distinguished experts from a variety of disciplines and professions. The sources for the ideas presented in this volume were (1) a series of dialogues with prominent educators and representatives of business, research associations, press and government; and (2) a review of some of the available literature.*

A conscious effort was made to ensure that as wide a variety of viewpoints as possible was represented in the study. The political spectrum from conservative to liberal thought was covered both in the dialogues and in the literature. The educators represented a range of widely differing disciplines — sociology and anthropology, political science and history, economics and labor-management relations, psychology and business administration. And a similar range of occupations, disciplines and viewpoints was included in the literature search. All told, therefore, this study has been able to draw upon the recent ideas of upwards of 150 of this country's best thinkers.

There are obvious difficulties inherent in any attempt to synthesize the views of so many and such diverse authorities with differing backgrounds, specialities and orientation. While this is a "view of the future" as they see it, it is not a collection of separate summaries of individual interviews and readings. The study attempted to draw together separate but related threads and weave them into new and meaningful patterns. The aim has, of course, been to preserve the meaning and intent of the original author, but in the synthesizing process a new element has been added — the judgment and perspective of the synthesizer: not, it should be added, his view of the future, but his view of the relationships among individual ideas and predictions.

The question then arises as to the weight of opinion behind any specific prediction. In fact, the chapter "Developing Trends" represents a broad consensus of predictions on forces at work in society in general, cutting across all institutions. Explicitly or implicitly,

---

*See Appendices A and B for a detailed listing of these sources.

a clear majority of authorities identified each one of these trends as one of the most significant future developments from their point of view. Thus, the higher educational standards of our population might be noted by a political scientist in terms of changing patterns of voting or of higher government expenditures on schools and colleges; by a labor economist or labor-management expert in terms of their impact on union structure and membership; and by a psychologist in terms of changes in an educated person's self-image and attitudes toward work. In general, the trend <u>identification</u> was not colored by the political or economic beliefs of the interviewees: differing <u>attitudes</u> to the trends were manifest, and differing <u>policy implications</u> might be drawn, but there was general agreement on the basic <u>facts</u> of the developing trends. It can be taken for granted, therefore, that there is really substantial support among those surveyed for the predictions made in this section of the study.

In the chapter on "Changing Institutions" the volume — though not the quality — of support on each item necessarily diminishes. This stems from the fact that comments on a specific institution — government, unions, business, etc. — tended to come only or mainly from those whose special interests lie in that area. However, while the number of supporting predictions might be smaller, the weighting of more expert knowledge should be considered in evaluating these statements. On balance, it seems likely that these predictions have approximately the same degree of validity as those on general societal trends.

It must be borne in mind, then, that these predictions are essentially those of the people we have talked with and whose works we have read, not those of the General Electric Company. However, we believe that they do provide a sound basis for establishing an environmental forecasting system, always remembering that this is but one phase of the system, and that the real payoff is to be found only in the successful deduction of business implications and the influencing of business plans.

2

THE INTERNATIONAL CONTEXT

In the opening chapter we pointed out that the principal focus of our study has been the future domestic environment, principally because our resources did not permit a broader scope. Even if this limitation had not been imposed, however, it might have been considered the better part of prudence to concentrate this experimental work in an area of greatest familiarity.

Yet it would have been ill advised to view the United States as an island untouched by the tides of world events. Such an insularity would have been almost literally unthinkable at a time when one of the major trends in American business is a great "turning outwards" toward world markets, coinciding with an invasion of the domestic market by overseas competitors.

So, while this discussion of world-wide events cannot pretend to be exhaustive, it does provide the international context within which future domestic events, described in the following chapters, will take place. It is merely indicative of some major assumptions concerning the larger environment, which is expected to be characterized by the development of four major trends:

1. Maintenance of the basic international power structure;
2. Continued economic growth, despite a conflict between population growth and economic development in the emerging nations;
3. The emergence of Japan as the third major power;
4. Polarization of main world tension on a North-South ("haves" versus "have-nots") axis rather than an East-West (Communist versus capitalist) axis.

 STABILITY AND FERMENT IN
THE INTERNATIONAL SYSTEM

Over-all, the international scene will be influenced by a mixture of elements of stability and elements of ferment in the decade ahead. While the odds are against any major upheavals or surprises in this period, it is certain that the problems associated with accelerating change, economic development, nationalism and political power plays will give rise to a climate of virtually uninterrupted tension.

If one were to draw up a prospective balance sheet showing elements of stability and ferment, it might be expected to show the following entries:

Elements of Stability

(a) There will be a marked lessening of the chances of direct military conflict among the developed nations; and it will be these nations that will control the power and the main flow of events. For the most part they are content with their present boundaries and show little sign of the old Junker or Samurai spirit. There will, of course, continue to be bitterly contested problems — notably those of a divided Germany — but there will be little or no inclination to resolve these problems by force. In part, this restraint stems from the possession of nuclear weaponry which tends to dampen, rather than enlarge, a nation's appetite for conflict. The limitations on the actual exercise of superpower capability

14

became transparently — and, for Americans, frustratingly — obvious during the Vietnam war.

(b) There is a growing recognition, on the part of both developed and developing nations, that the best formula for wealth, power and prestige in tomorrow's world will be economic and technological growth, not military conquest. Virtually every government has made a national commitment to continuing as high a rate of economic growth as possible, recognizing this as not only a means of ensuring domestic progress and stability but also the real basis for ranking in the international power structure.

(c) A further stabilizing force will be the world-wide spread of the Twentieth Century characteristics of urbanization and industrialization. Not only will improved transportation and communication techniques accent human proximity and awareness, but also much of the technology and many of the habits, attitudes and institutions of the urban-industrial complex will become common features of developed and developing nations alike. Cities around the globe will manifest the signs of what may be termed a "single world civilization," superimposed on cultural differences of the nations. The stabilizing effect of this commonality of urban-industrial interests should not, of course, be overstated. Indeed, within individual countries, urban and industrial problems can be profoundly disruptive as they become acute. However, these shared interests and shared experience among countries tend to place a premium on preserving a reasonably stable framework of international order within which problems can be resolved and trade promoted.

(d) A growing economic interdependence among nations, marked by an increased exchange of goods, technology, money and personnel, will tend to obsolete some of the old political boundaries and idealogical divisions. For instance, while the "convergence theory" (which postulates a growing similarity between communism and capitalism to a point where they are virtually indistinguishable) is generally rejected, there is agreement that we shall see an increasing accommodation between East and West based on a search for an acceptable economic and political modus vivendi. Then

15

again, the evolving regional groupings in Europe, Latin America and Southeast Asia will start to impose a new set of economic realities transcending boundaries based on purely political and national considerations.

Elements of Ferment

(a) Nationalism, however, will be a strong — and, over the short term at least, a growing — force to reckon with in capitalist, Communist and uncommitted nations alike. The chauvinism associated with newly won political independence in the developing nations and the inherent problems of progress toward free trade and regional economies will serve to reinforce the effects of nationalism. The protectionist reaction in the United States to the negotiation of Kennedy Round tariff reductions was symptomatic of this underlying tension between national interests and international trade.

Politically speaking, the bipolar world will give way to a multipolar world (though in terms of economic and, more especially, military power the world will continue on a bipolar basis). Monolithic blocs, under a rigid hegemony of a superpower, will be a thing of the past. The secondary powers are already in a state of revolt against the tutelage of the superpowers, as negotiations on the nuclear non-proliferation treaty and Communist nations' varying reaction to the invasion of Czechoslovakia have made abundantly clear.

(b) Tensions arising in the developing nations from problems of economic development and the simultaneous breakdown of both colonial and tribal forms of government will be a major source of unrest. Although their lack of world power and posture should keep these troubles localized (or, at worst, regionalized), the major problem will come from the interaction of this unrest with big-power rivalries. If, as seems inevitable, the constant crisis of the underdeveloped world continues, there will always be a chance of it sparking a wider conflict through the intervention of one of the major powers.

(c) China will retain the potential for causing instability either by direct aggression or, more likely, by sponsoring "wars of national liberation." However, this potential is likely to be severely restricted over the short- to mid-term, as her economy struggles to recover from the twin disasters of the Cultural Revolution and the Great Leap Forward. Then, too, China's political and diplomatic influence, even in the underdeveloped world, will remain at a low ebb for some time, as a result of the serious rebuffs she suffered in 1966-1967 in Africa and Asia. Both Chinese missions and Peking-sponsored Communist parties have thus far failed to accommodate their programs to the nationalist spirit of the developing nations. If China does succeed in harnessing these forces, and in overcoming her domestic problems, her future actions may well become as aggressive as her present words.

There is also the possibility that China's aggressive struggle for leadership in the Communist world might lead to a showdown with the U.S.S.R. or provoke Russian military leaders to a preemptive strike. The possibility of an "accidental" war or of a situation getting suddenly out of control cannot, of course, be entirely discounted. But, these contingencies aside, the consensus of informed thought seems to be that, for the Seventies at least, China will not have the capability and Russia will have neither the inclination nor real need to wage a nuclear war over this rivalry.

(d) There will be a constant danger of nuclear proliferation despite U.S.-U.S.S.R. desire for non-proliferation. With China in possession of a nuclear armory, Japan may not long remain satisfied with the protection offered by an American ABM system and sometime in the 1970's may seek her own nuclear balance with China. Once the non-proliferation wall has been breached, other nations may seek big-power status for themselves by developing nuclear capability.

The Prospects for Equilibrium

On balance, then, the international system — which will continue to be predominately a nation-state system — is likely to undergo fewer abrupt and cataclysmic changes in the next decade than it has in the post-World War II period (e.g., the emergence of nuclear power; the end of colonialism and break-up of empires; the birth of many new Asiatic and African nations). And the basic power structure is expected to remain substantially as it is now, with the U.S. and Soviet Union continuing in their roles as superpowers, followed by Japan, West Germany, France, the United Kingdom and China (probably in that order), with Italy, Canada and India in the ranks of intermediate powers.

It is a reasonable hypothesis that the U.S. and U.S.S.R. will seek to preserve the basic economic-political equilibrium whenever it is seriously threatened. Although national interests will continue to bring these superpowers into economic and political competition, they recognize the need to maintain an acceptable degree of stability in their relationships. The validity of this hypothesis has been tested in a variety of circumstances in the past decade, from the Cuban missile crisis, to the Middle East, to the Soviet intervention in Czechoslovakia. Most notably in this last episode, despite the initial strong reactions on both sides, within a relatively few months the two powers had resumed progress toward nuclear non-proliferation, cooperation in space and strategic arms limitation talks (SALT).

This hypothesis does not, however, exclude the possibility (even the probability) of the U.S.S.R. exploiting whatever openings present themselves for enlarging her sphere of influence, whenever she thinks she can profitably and safely do so. It does suggest that such exploitation will not be pressed to the point of rupturing the modus vivendi with the United States.

Within the over-all stability of the international framework, however, there will be the prolonged uncertainty of local or regional tension and conflict among the smaller powers. In many ways, peace will be even harder to manage in a multipolar world than it was in the bipolar world of the Cold War Fifties.

Czechoslovakia — a Straw in the Wind?

It is instructive to examine some of these projections in the light of a single major dramatic development — the Soviet intervention (along with East German, Polish, Hungarian and Bulgarian troops) in Czechoslovakia to redress what were seem as inadmissible revisionist policies of the Dubcek regime in that country. On its face, this development appeared to run counter to the projections of not resolving problems by force and of a developing East-West accommodation. However, the consequences of that invasion — both within the Communist bloc and in East-West relations — are still unfolding.

One of the more noteworthy repercussions has been the dissension this act has caused in the Communist camp. While four East European countries sent troop contingents to support the invasion, the Rumanians and Yugoslavs bitterly denounced the action (possibly fearing similar moves against their countries), as did the Communist parties in, for example, Italy and France. Even in the Soviet Union public disagreement was expressed. In a remarkable document, "Thoughts about Progress, Peaceful Co-existence and Intellectual Freedom," the Soviet physicist Andrei D. Sakharov wrote:

> ...the world's Communists will also view negatively any at-tempts to revive Stalinism. . . . Today the key to a progressive restructuring of the system of government in the interests of mankind lies in intellectual freedom. This has been understood, in particular, by the Czechoslovaks <u>and there can be no doubt that we should support their bold initiative</u>, which is so valuable for the future of socialism and all mankind. (Emphasis added.)

And, of course, within Czechoslovakia itself popular support for economic reforms and press freedom and opposition to Soviet restrictions and censorship continue to be overwhelming.

Both in the Communist camp and within the Soviet Union itself, therefore, the reaction to the invasion has been in line with certain predicted and continuing world-wide trends — nationalism, independence and a rejection of authoritarianism. The Brezhnev doctrine of a "socialist commonwealth" — seeking both to define communism more rigidly and to assert the principle that, once a country has established a Communist regime, it will not be allowed to stray from the Communist fold — has, not surprisingly, met with strong opposition; and Soviet influence in the international Communist movement has been reduced to its lowest point in fifty years. The strength of these trends is likely to grow rather than diminish. For the immediate future, Russia will be hampered by involvement in what has been described as "her political Vietnam," able neither to withdraw without loss of prestige and influence nor to attain fully her original objective of a "normalization" of the Czech regime. The movement toward polycentrism in the Communist world will, thus, most probably be a continuing feature of the international political scene.

The Czechoslovakian episode and its consequences have also highlighted an internal contradiction in the Soviet system. It is generally agreed that the U.S.S.R. is entering a period of political crisis, with a conservative regime in uneasy power, seeking to preserve stability at the expense of flexibility and placing a high premium on ideological unity. The decision to intervene in Czechoslovakia was clearly not a unanimous one, and the subsequent handling of Czech resistance further underscored divisions in Soviet leadership. At the same time, the world-wide forces of education and technology are giving rise to an intellectual and technocratic elite that is inclined to be less dogmatic, less ideological and less bureaucratic than the old party system.

The Sakharov document, the Daniel-Sinyavsky trials, the demonstrations led by the younger Litvinov are all indicative of developing tensions between the old system and what Milovan Djilas has called the "new class." Because the system is not open and adaptive to gradual change, some observers foresee the possibility that these internal tensions may build up to the point of a violent convulsion in Russia (and East Germany and Poland, which also have conservative, repressive regimes). Whether such a convulsion does take place, or a more gradual change evolves despite the current regime's desire to "keep the lid on," the Czechoslovakian intervention may be seen in retrospect as a critical point at which internal opposition started to gain real momentum.

At the same time this relatively weak and divided leadership could prove dangerous in its impact on U.S.-U.S.S.R. relationships. Some analysts have assessed the Soviet action in Czechoslovakia as setting East-West cooperation back five years, and the London Economist observed that it could mean "a lot more ice on the barbed wire of Europe in the 1970's." On the other hand, as we have already noted, in the U.S. the nuclear non-proliferation treaty — held up by immediate reaction to the Soviet invasion — has been ratified by the Senate; and some progress is being maintained toward cooperation in space programs and U.S.-U.S.S.R. talks on moderating, if not reducing, the level of strategic armaments development. Thus, while there have been indications that the predicted accommodation between East and West may not proceed smoothly or rapidly, there remains substantial validation of the long-term trend toward a political and economic accommodation.

As is the case with many other trends, this will not be a uniform or uninterrupted trend: it will be, rather, the product of the push and pull of many conflicting forces. Indeed, it seems indisputable that there will be many signs of both rivalry and accommodation between the two superpowers in the Seventies. While competition may be the dominant theme, it seems likely to be kept within bounds and certainly to be prevented from developing into a serious threat to the basic political and economic equilibrium.

2. ECONOMIC GROWTH

One of the most significant trends of the post-World War II period — the sustained economic growth in so many nations — is expected to continue through the next ten years and beyond. There are many reasons for believing that recent history has not witnessed just a temporary spurt in growth rates, and that recent trends will become the new long-term growth trends. The "international gamesmanship" in economic growth comparisons plus the recognition that, for the long term, political power (to paraphrase Mao Tse Tung) grows out of a barrel of economic goods, merely provide the psychological and political impetus behind more tangible forces.

In 1970, the research and development explosion is little more than twenty years old: it is essentially a post-World War II phenomenon. While the exponential growth in research and development expenditures in the most advanced countries must soon be moderated, there is every reason to believe that the main benefits of this revolution still lie ahead of us. Two statements that have gained popular currency are: "90 percent of all the scientists and engineers who have ever lived are alive today;" and "Half of all the R&D expenditures made in the U.S. since its founding have occurred in the last five to six years."

The facts behind these statements strengthen the probability of this prospective payoff. Clearly, it is the already developed nations that will be the prime beneficiaries of this trend; but there is a great and growing body of exportable technology that can be assimilated by the developing economies.

In varying ways, and at differing levels of sophistication, the management and education revolutions will contribute to the growth process. The contribution that will be made, in developed countries, by computerization and systems planning can be equalled (if not surpassed, relatively speaking), in a less sophisticated economy, by simpler management techniques for greater productivity. The growth payoff from improved education is most marked: a 1962 study by Edward F. Denison showed that the rising educational level of the work force had contributed 23 percent to the U.S. growth rate.* In most of the new nations the process of universal education is just getting started; and, while this process has been virtually completed in developing countries, the payoff from improvements and extension of the educational system is expected to continue.

The commonly accepted use of governmental fiscal and monetary policy in developed countries to counter potential cycles in business activity, and significant structural changes in advanced economies,

---

*"The Sources of Economic Growth in the United States and the Alternatives Before Us" (Supplementary Paper No. 13 published by the Committee for Economic Development).

will moderate the depressive effect on business confidence and help to stimulate a bolder and more sustained investment in new capital equipment. This steadier pace of economic growth will also tend to stabilize markets for the developing nations' raw materials, although the terms of trade may well continue on an adverse course for these nations due to the inflated prices they will have to pay for imported industrial goods.

Despite this general recognition that governments can help promote stability and growth, there will be a trend away from central economic decision-making. Over-all state planning will continue, but a general trend is expected toward more and more private or decentralized production and consumption, even in less developed countries (LDC's) and Communist nations.

A further stimulus to growth will be provided by the formation of common markets and the reduction of tariffs (accompanied by new sources of international liquidity to finance increased world trade). The Latin American countries are working toward a common market in the 1980s: in Europe, Britain's entry into the European Economic Community is expected in three to five years, with an eventual merger of EEC with most of the European Free Trade Association countries. If the recent growth experience of EEC and the Central American Common Market is projected into the future of these and similar regional economic groupings, the spur to development will clearly be considerable.

Economic growth in the LDC's will be hobbled by their disproportionate share of population growth. In the industrialized nations, a steady decline in the death rate has, in most cases, been accompanied by a lowering of the birth rate (though population as a whole does, of course, continue to grow). In the LDC's, however, the higher birth rates characteristic of agricultural societies have continued, while there have been dramatic and sudden reductions in death rates due to the rapid application of modern medical science. The result has been the "population explosion" that will see the LDC's share of world population climb from 68 percent to 75 percent by the end of the century. An accentuated impact of this explosive growth will be felt in the cities to which the unemployed youth of the villages will move: a national population growth rate of 3 percent a year can thus easily be translated into a 15 percent growth rate in urban areas.

Although birth rates are expected to be somewhat lower than current levels — world population in 2000 is now predicted at a 6.4 billion level versus a figure of 7.2 billion on the basis of straight-line projections — LDC's struggling toward an economic "take-off" will have to struggle even harder to increase per capita production and income.

The net effect of all these forces is expected to be growth in per capita GNP on the order of 3.5 percent a year in the more developed countries, and 2.8 percent in the LDC's.

The prospects for an increase in East-West trade are so qualified that this is likely to be a neutral element so far as contribution to economic growth rates is concerned. Western European countries, in their aggressive search for new markets outside EEC, will step up their efforts to develop Communist markets for their manufactured goods, but a low ceiling will be imposed on the volume of this trade by the Communists' limited ability to supply goods needed by the West. Unless Russia and the Communist bloc countries are prepared to incur sizable adverse trade balances with the West, their imports of finished goods will, by and large, be limited by the West's demand for the East's raw materials.

These factors will also be determinative in limiting U.S. trade with the East. In addition, the policy of extending to Communist nations the long-term credits they seek will remain a politically unacceptable feature and serve to dampen even further the prospects for any significant increase in this trading.

Prospects for the International Monetary System

The two years of this study's progress saw an almost uninterrupted series of crises in the international monetary field — a devaluation of the British pound; a drastic worsening (in the fourth quarter of 1967) in the U.S. balance of payments; the gold crisis and introduction of the two-price system; uncertainty over the Canadian dollar (and, again, over the pound); and, finally, the run on the franc in the face of a strengthening mark, leading to a French devaluation in the fall of 1969. Yet the original study mentioned only the problem of intensified foreign competition, inflation, high interest rates and a world-wide capital shortage, while predicting the introduction of new sources of international liquidity to finance increased world trade.

Clearly, maintenance of a basic equilibrium (not rigidity) in the international monetary system is a fundamental requirement for economic development and growth in world trade. The absence of any mention of this factor in the interviews can scarcely be due to oversight of this crucial factor, but rather to an unspoken assumption that in this field — as in nuclear war — a final crisis, undermining the whole system, would not come.

And indeed, despite the recurrent problems and tensions in the system, there is much evidence to support both this assumption and the identification of basic problems. Certainly, a principal cause of monetary crises has been the fact that the economies of the major industrial nations have been (and seem likely to remain) inflation-prone. Committed to policies of full employment, these governments have shown an understandable reluctance, when economies become over-heated, to take steps that might lead to deflation and so to a politically unacceptable increase in unemployment. As a result, inflation tends to persist and currencies get out of whack on the international exchange markets. Then, since the Bretton Woods Agreement prescribes a policy of fixed exchange rates, these maladjustments cannot be fully reflected in the markets, and distortions are allowed to build up to near-crisis proportions.

Since inflation is generally predicted to continue as a feature of the international economic scene, and since commitment to full employment policies is scarcely likely to decrease, we must expect that the potential for such periodic crises will persist. Yet these same nations have recognized the need to preserve the system and maintain an equilibrium at almost any cost. This has been revealed in the multilateral support for the pound; then in devising the expedient of a two-price system for gold; and then again in the negotiations surrounding the franc-mark confrontation. So it would appear that there is a reasonable basis for the assumption that these crises will be kept manageable and not allowed to disrupt completely the processes of economic growth and world trade.

Meanwhile, the search to improve manageability of the system will continue. On the one hand, the agreements to introduce Special Drawing Rights as a means of increasing reserves will be implemented in the immediate future. On the other hand, some modification of the adjustment process is likely to be made eventually, though maybe not for five or so years. While proposals to let exchange rates float freely would encounter insuperable opposition from monetary officials interested in preserving as much stability as possible, more moderate suggestions for flexibility are more likely to gain acceptance.

The most probable solution in this area would seem to be a system of allowing exchange rates to fluctuate within a broader band (say, 2 percent — rather than the present 1 percent — on either side of parity), combined with provision for more frequent, but smaller changes in parity (the "crawling peg" concept).

Within the over-all problem, the U.S. position has been, and will continue to be, a central one because of the dollar's role as a key source of liquidity. Notwithstanding the fact that the U.S. balance of payments was in surplus in 1968, the extent of the trouble is revealed in the decline in the gold stock and, most dramatically, in the drastic reduction of the merchandise trade balance to $626 million (compared with $3,860 million in 1967). Clearly a key task in efforts to maintain international monetary equilibrium over the next few years will be that of bringing domestic inflation under control. Given the degree of public and political reluctance to accept much of a rise in the unemployment rate, the most that can be hoped for on this front is a gradual slowing-down of the inflationary drive. This, in turn, suggests a period of intensified competition with overseas suppliers and hard bargaining over the size of salary, wage and benefit increases.

 RISE OF JAPAN

Within the predicted stability of the international power structure, the most important shift in power will, in all likelihood, come from the "second rise" of Japan. At a time when most of the world has a "China obsession," the prospect that her neighbor to the east will become the most important power in the Orient — and the third power in the world — seems generally overlooked.

This development stems from the fact (mentioned earlier) that international standing will, in the main, be a factor of economic capabilities (i.e., resources plus the ability to marshal and utilize them effectively). With her population growth under control, with a well-trained work force, and acquiring technological and scientific capabilities to match those of any of the current industrial leaders, Japan's economy seems likely to grow at rates of 7 to 10 percent a year for the foreseeable future. Japan has already moved ahead of West Germany to become the world's number three economic power, surpassed only by the United States and U.S.S.R. The most startling fact is that, if this growth rate were to persist till the year 2000, Japan would then surpass even the U.S.A. in per capita GNP.

The translation of this economic capability into political influence is a logical consequence. Already Japan is on the brink of creating a sphere of influence for herself in the vacuum left by China's rebuff in Indonesia and introversion due to the Cultural Revolution, while India is badly weakened by population and economic problems. The Japanese show every sign of being able to overcome the stigma of their aggression in the Thirties and Forties, and of exercising leadership in the underdeveloped world by the example of their economic success, by financial and technological aid and (perhaps above all) by being non-white.

It is, at the moment at least, an open question whether there will be political and diplomatic competition between Japan and the U.S.A. to match the economic competition that has already occurred. Most probably by the mid-1970's, Japan's foreign aid program will outstrip the United States', and this fact alone will increase her

27

influence among the "third world" nations which might otherwise have relied mainly on American or European aid for their economic development.

However, the prospects for a political confrontation between the two powers are lessened by the fact that U.S. reaction to its involvement in Vietnam will lead to a scaling-down of its world commitments. Not only will there be a marked reluctance to become involved in similar wars in the future, but there is likely to be a redefinition of U.S. foreign policy in narrower terms of self-interest. As a result, more reliance would be placed on multi-national approaches to economic and political stability than on single-handed action by the United States. In this case we might well see a growing number of multilateral aid programs with the U.S.A. and Japan in partnership rather than confrontation.

4. "NORTH-SOUTH" POLARIZATION

The effect of the population and economic growth rates postulated earlier will be to increase rather than decrease the dichotomy between the LDC's and the more developed countries. We shall see an inevitable polarization of these two groups (roughly equivalent to a North-South division of the world)* that will be far more lasting and significant than that between Communist and capitalist economies.

The salient statistics, leading to the widening gap during the final third of this century, tell the story in the following table:

The Growing "North-South" Economic Gap

	1965		2000	
	% of World Population	GNP Per Capita	% of World Population	GNP Per Capita
Less Developed Countries . . .	68%	$135	75%	$325
More Developed Countries . . .	32%	$1,675	25%	$5,775

Source: "The Year 2000: A Framework for Speculation on the Next Thirty-three Years," by Herman Kahn and Anthony J. Weiner

*In fact, the comparison is made here between North America, Europe, Japan and Australia/New Zealand on the one hand, and South America, Asia and Africa (including South Africa) on the other.

28

Thus, while per capita performance of the LDC's will more than double, the gap will be half again as big as it is now between the two groups (i.e., the LDC's will fall from one-twelfth to one-eighteenth of the level of the advanced economies).

One consequence of this economic differential may be a shift in the focus of U.S. foreign policy from Europe to preventing an eventual "international race war." Although it is virtually impossible to envisage such a war occurring within the timespan of this study's forecasts, it is far from unlikely that frustration and despair might eventually build up to a point where one of the LDC's (China herself, or another country with China's aid) might be tempted to launch a suicidal attack on a developed country — especially if cheap nuclear weapons were then available. At that point in the polarization, we may well find the U.S. and U.S.S.R. in a precarious and informal "alliance," upholding the needs and rights of the affluent third of the world against the demands of the economically deprived two-thirds.

In its attempt to deal with this problem, the United States will encounter a number of actual or potential dangers:

(a) That the vastness of the problem could create a feeling of helplessness at our inability to solve it, and thus give rise to a neo-isolationism;

(b) That a new form of economic colonialism could emerge;

(c) That we could become involved in a series of inter-LDC wars (in Africa, Asia and Latin America), and exhaust our resources, energy and will, as Rome did, in frontier wars. Already, we have been involved in three major wars in Asia in the past twenty-five years.

These might be summed up as the dangers of under- or over-involvement: but the United States and other developed nations will have to face up to them because some form of involvement (through the transfer of economic, educational and technological assistance) is inevitable. And it will be inevitable because, to paraphrase Lincoln, the world cannot endure permanently, half affluent and half deprived.

3

DEVELOPING TRENDS

The processes of social change, particularly in a society as large and diverse as the United States, are infinitely varied and complex. Many forces will be at work at any given time, each with its own characteristics and course, each interacting with the others, sometimes at variance, sometimes supportive and strengthening.

To attempt to impose a single pattern on such a shifting kaleidoscope of change may, therefore, have the appearance of an exercise in futility or even of being quite misleading. Yet a simple enumeration and description of multitudinous pieces of change cannot be said to constitute a systematic analysis of the environment. Some more sophisticated attempt must be made to segregate the major forces for change and to analyze their impact on, and relationships with, each other. Only in such a way can we begin to make sense of change.

This study has interpreted social change in the United States over the next ten years as the interaction of eight significant forces for change:

1. Increasing affluence
2. Economic stabilization
3. Rising tide of education
4. Changing attitudes toward work and leisure
5. Growing interdependence of institutions
6. Emergence of the "post-industrial" society
7. Strengthening of pluralism and individualism
8. The urban/minority problem

Some of these forces are not, of course, new with the Seventies: social forces are not constrained by neat classification into decades. Increasing affluence and education have, indeed, been a feature of the American scene for most of this century. However, it must be remembered that, when an old trend continues to have force as an agent of social change, its future implications can still be novel, almost revolutionary. As in a nuclear pile a slight change can make the whole mass go critical, so a relatively small difference in degree in a social force can lead to a difference in kind in its effects.

1.   INCREASING AFFLUENCE

There are, of course, many standards by which one can measure affluence, and all the usual economic indicators are projected to show substantial increases. In the fifteen year period from 1965 to 1980, for instance, we can expect roughly a 50 percent increase, in real terms, in both median family income (from $7,000 to $10,450) and per capita disposable income (from $2,400 to $3,600). Such an increase, coming on top of what is already (by world standards) unheard-of affluence, must have some far-reaching consequences in terms of changing spending habits, markets and economic attitudes.

Such gains would not, of course, mean the eradication of poverty, for they are not likely to be spread evenly over all segments of the population. Indeed, in absolute terms, the gap between some groups will widen rather than narrow. Thus, while non-whites will see their per capita income grow, in the ten years ending in 1975, faster than that of whites (40 versus 30 percent), they will fall further

32

behind in actual dollars — $1,250 versus $2,300 in 1965 (a difference of $1,050); $1,750 versus $2,980 in 1975 (a difference of $1,230). Nevertheless, more and more individuals and families will move into middle-class status, leaving the poor a smaller, but more visible, class.

A logical result of such a movement would be a growing similarity in our basic standard of living, with some narrowing of the differences between levels of expenditures on such essentials as food, clothing, housing, medical attention and education. Increasing percentages of discretionary income would be spent on such things as travel, leisure and cultural and "self-improvement" activities. In total, these expenditures would represent a change, not merely in spending habits, but (more significantly) in way of life.

Levels of per capita affluence would receive part of their boost from the expected decline in birth rates from the high levels of the late Forties and Fifties. As we enter the Seventies, both the birth rate and the fertility rate are hovering around the low levels reached during the Depression; and, though predictions of birth rates are notoriously uncertain, these low rates seem likely to persist throughout the decade. This trend seems to be due not so much to improved birth control methods as to a conscious search for a different quality in living — a different family lifestyle, and a greater awareness of the social consequences of the population explosion.*

Another attitudinal shift expected from greater affluence is a developing public impatience with all forms of economic hardships. In part, this attitude would derive from the fact that many of these hardships (e.g., poverty) seem on the brink of being reduced to manageable proportions, in part, from a feeling that such hardships are not consonant with the "quality of life" that is being sought. The

---

*Total population will, of course, continue to grow, though at a slower rate than might otherwise have been the case. Because our population base is so large, even a 1 percent growth rate will produce a "population explosion" of more than two million extra people each year. It is worth noting that there is emerging a school of thought that questions the advisability of even this lower growth rate (because of its pressure on resources, environmental problems, etc.) and advocates a conscious national policy of "zero population growth."

A Lower Frustation Tolerance: Some Developing
Public Reactions

- "Poverty? It's an anomaly in an affluent nation. If someone really can't find employment — and is 'untrainable' — we should guarantee him an income."

- "Unemployment? We ought to be able to manage the economy better so that anyone willing and able to work has a job — even if the government has to step in and create jobs. If someone is temporarily unemployed, through no fault of his, we should just about take all the hardship out of his 'between-jobs' period."

- "Sickness? A serious and unexpected illness can be one of the cruelest blows of fate for an individual and a family, and the risk-insurance should be borne communally. Besides, if a nation's most precious resources are its people, health is properly a matter of national concern."

- "Retirement? Why should a good worker have to take a severe cut in income when he retires? Pensions and Social Security should enable him to maintain his standard of living."

- "Strikes? They're an uncivilized way of settling disputes and should be restricted — especially if we are to manage our economy successfully."

hypothetical quotations cited in the box above project the probable public response to ways of dealing with these problems: taken together, they give some idea of the future scope of this attitude.

Many of these public reactions have been around, in some form, for twenty or thirty years, but there is nothing on the social horizon to suggest that they have yet run their full course. Rather, the signs are that we should expect a lower frustration tolerance with respect to anything that impairs an individual's ability to work, live in decency (judged by current standards of society) and express himself. The general feeling will be that we should do whatever can be done to remove these economic hardships or blocks, and that, in the process, determination of "what can be done" should not be made by reference to strict economic criteria alone. In these, as in other matters, we should be prepared for a growing belief that an affluent society can afford the luxury of some departure from short-term economic efficiency as the main determinant of social policies and programs.

In somewhat similar vein, affluence is creating a "generation gap" in attitudes toward money. To the older generation which grew up in the Depression or even in the Forties, a paycheck was a highly prized possession, and money was valued all the higher for being hard to come by. To the middle-class generation of tomorrow, accustomed to high and constantly increasing wage and salary levels, money will be much more taken for granted, much less of a motivator and relegated to the category of "means" rather than "ends." This is not to say that money will be unimportant (except for a relatively few idealists); only that, in psychological terms, it is more likely to be a "dissatisfier" rather than a "satisfier," i.e., its absence can cause dissatisfaction, but its presence will not satisfy a person's most important motivational needs.

2. ECONOMIC STABILIZATION

There is now widespread agreement on the prediction of a further
flattening of the business cycle. Whereas in the fifteen years, 1949
to 1964, the unemployment rate had a five-point swing, from a low
of 2.5 percent to a high of 7.5 percent, the next fifteen years may
see the swing kept within a 1 to 1.5 point range, at a level of about
3 to 4.5 percent.* Again, whereas post-World War II recessions
have averaged 10 percent cutbacks in industrial production, future
declines are expected to be only half as deep. The over-all growth
rate over a five- or ten-year period may not be changed as a consequence of this development, but the year-to-year fluctuations are
predictably going to be smaller.

From the business planning point of view, a clear distinction must
be drawn between the micro-economic and macro-economic implications of this trend. A general over-all stabilization of the economy
does not preclude the possibility of sectoral booms and busts. In
1966, for instance, over-all GNP continued to rise, but residential
housing starts fell by more than one-third. So any individual business may still be subject to relatively large swings in the size of its
market or in its share of that market. However, its planning will
still be influenced by the macro-economic forces accompanying this
trend, including the role of government policies in the economy, the
potential for inflationary pressure, tight labor markets and competition for capital resources.

Such stabilization — or moderation of the business cycle — would
be due only in part to the impact of governmental policies. It is true
that "large-scale" unemployment (probably defined as 5—6 percent in
the light of new public expectations) has become too great a political

---

*This prediction is made despite the fact that, between 1965 and
1975, the United States will experience the largest increase in its labor force for any ten year period in our history. The apparent anomaly
of tight labor markets in a period of great labor force growth is ex-
plained by (1) the political necessity of avoiding the criticism of creating a recession; (2) the great growth in public and private demand;
and (3) the projected structural changes in the economy (see below).

liability for any administration to tolerate for long. It is also true that there is general acceptance of the contracyclical use of fiscal and monetary policy: the debates now concern only the extent, timing and mix of policy changes.

While inflation has emerged in recent years as the prime economic problem, it is evident that efforts to solve or moderate the problem will not be made at the expense of a substantially higher unemployment rate. Unemployment has now been at or below the 4 percent rate for so long that public expectations will in the future be at a new, and lower, level in this regard. Neither Democratic nor Republican administrations will be prepared to accept the political liability of allowing unemployment to rise more than a few percentage points, certainly not above the 4.5 percent figure now predicted to be the upper limit of the range. Indeed, several government programs, such as manpower training and unemployment compensation, now have this figure proposed as a "trigger point" at which additional resources will be brought in to alleviate and reverse the situation.

However, there are structural changes, too, that will determine a more stable course for the economy. Among those identified as having special influence on future performance (because they will themselves be expanding factors) are:

(a) Technology and automation, with their involvement of long-range programs and large, fixed overhead costs, which place a premium on stable production, near optimum operating rates;

(b) Computerized inventory control, which will reduce the relative size of inventories and help dampen (not eliminate) the past, wide fluctuations in the inventory-sales ratio;

(c) The changing structure of the labor force, with the major growth in the traditionally more stable employment sectors of white-collar workers and the services, trade and government occupations;

(d) Narrowing of the differential between paying a man to produce and paying him on layoff, as layoffs become more costly (through higher unemployment compensation and expanded SUB-type programs). Thus, the traditionally variable direct labor costs will become less variable, making a further incentive for stable employment and production.

Business confidence, too, seems more durably optimistic, as its long-term planning and investment policies make evident. Hitherto this has been counted as a potent but volatile influence in the economy; but now more and more businessmen seem to believe — and act on the belief — that future growth will be more stable and more assured. There is a feeling that ours will be a much more "self-conscious" economy and so a more manageable one (through private as well as governmental planning). Though problems will be well in evidence (e.g., inflationary threats and tight labor markets), more and more businessmen are expected to be willing to plan production and capital investment programs with greater confidence in the prospect of a more stable growth pattern.

3. RISING TIDE OF EDUCATION

Like affluence, education is not a new element on the American scene; but, also like affluence, its impact on social change will continue to grow, both in material terms and in patterns of living and thinking.

In purely tangible terms we should anticipate an increasing percentage of students completing high school and going on to college; a great growth of junior colleges; much higher public and private expenditures for education due to inflated salary schedules, lower pupil-teacher ratios and investments in computer-assisted instruction and other new materials and methods. Within the next ten years we shall probably have established a norm of fourteen or fifteen years free education, with greatly expanded scholarship and loan funds to carry students beyond that to college. After this period of formal education, the process of learning and re-training is expected to continue throughout a person's career, leading to new programs and new relationships among business, unions, governments, schools, and universities to institutionalize this process.

As recently as the early Fifties we were spending on education an amount equal to some 3 percent of Gross National Product. Today that percentage has more than doubled; and so, of course, has GNP.

38

Predictably this figure will approach, and probably pass, the 10 percent mark by the end of the decade.

These physical manifestations are merely reflections of a new public attitude toward education and learning. Society is placing an increasing premium on more and better education in recognition of the fact that change demands versatility and flexibility; and these, in turn, demand even more education and a continuing flow of new knowledge. Education and knowledge have, of course, for centuries been important factors in society; but both the degree and the character of their importance are now changing fast.

Education, up till now, has been largely concerned with the transmission of accumulated knowledge and perpetuation of the culture. In other words, it could be said to have been largely concerned with maintaining and improving the status quo, so far as its impact on the majority of graduates was concerned. From now on, we are told, it will be more a process of developing skill in thought processes and of preparation for change. In the past, knowledge has consisted mainly of what has been termed "folk knowledge," practical information about observable and tangible phenomena. In the "post-industrial" era (see p. 46), Daniel Bell has written, "what has now become decisive for society is the new centrality of theoretical knowledge the primacy of theory over empiricism."* Though perhaps overstated, Bell's point nonetheless makes an interesting historical contrast.

This upgrading of the importance of education also results, in part, from a new way of looking at it: the period of formal schooling is increasingly being regarded as an "investment" rather than a "consumption" period, i.e., as a way of capitalizing time (which is, like land, our great unreproduceable asset). Individuals and families have, of course, long had this investment outlook: the notion of saving for the children's college education, to give them a good start in life, has been a very prevalent one. So far as public policy and spending have been concerned, however, public attitudes have inclined more to the consumption outlook as contrasted with the view of the

---

*"Notes on the post-industrial society (I)," The Public Interest, Winter, 1967, p. 28.

interstate highway program or of defense expenditures as an investment in security. Only recently have these attitudes begun to change
as a new scale of social priorities emerges.

In another way, too, education is viewed as a "revolutionary" force
— by changing people's self-image. The better educated person will
have more self-respect; will want to be treated more as an individual;
will be far less tolerant of authoritarianism* and organization restraints; will have different and higher expectations of what he wants
to put into a job and what he wants to get out of it. These attitudinal
changes will clearly be most marked among the college educated who
will form the managerial, professional and technical ranks of tomorrow; but they will increasingly (though perhaps more slowly) influence the thinking of the high school graduate who becomes a production or service worker.

In the structuring of work for such educated manpower, the technically perfect solution is likely not to be the best solution overall.
Job fragmentation may remain a necessity in work assignments for
unskilled workers newly absorbed into the labor force; but job enlargement may well be a sine qua non for holding the interest and
motivating the performance of tomorrow's college or high school
graduate.

Considering, then, all its implications — individual, institutional
and social — it is evident that education will be a force for change in
the United States even more than it will be, at a much simpler and
less sophisticated level, in the developing countries. To overlook its
continued impact on our society, merely because it is not a new force
for change, can be an open invitation to disorder and disruption, as
the college experience of recent years has amply demonstrated (see
pp. 9, 92–94).

---

*Internationally, too, the spread of universal education will make
totalitarian states more difficult to govern and lead to some relaxation of authoritarianism. Totalitarian states with a high level of
literacy, such as the U.S.S.R. and Poland, have experienced relatively greater restiveness among their people and have felt the
need to ease controls more than those with a low literacy level,
such as Bolivia and Albania.

4. CHANGING ATTITUDES TOWARD WORK AND LEISURE

Increasing affluence and rising education are bound, over the short term, to change people's attitudes toward work (as already indicated) and, over the longer term, could result in some erosion of traditional work values. The pace at which the long-term factor enters the short-term picture will depend in large part on the extent to which institutions in our society are able to structure meaningful (in the eyes of potential employees) goals and to make work a challenging and intellectually satisfying experience.

Up to this point in our history, our society has been dominated by the old Puritan concept of work — namely, that work is unavoidable; that it is, mostly, hard (done "in the sweat of thy face"); that it deals with "things"; and that it is a duty. In one respect, at least, this concept is already, and will increasingly be, out of touch with the real world. Productivity is such that our economy can produce all the "things" society needs with only a fraction of the total labor force. By 1980, little more than one-fifth of the labor force will be directly involved in manufacturing products, mining, growing crops, constructing buildings.*

Further, the notion that hard or unpleasant work must be tolerated because it is unavoidable is expected to enjoy less and less currency. Institutions will find that they simply cannot afford to pay the premium demanded for the performance of unpleasant work — a trend that will start with professional and technical personnel and then gradually pervade the ranks of skilled and unskilled workers.

Finally, the concept of work as a duty may be called into question. The first step in this direction has already been taken with the idea that both leisure and work are equally valid activities; that leisure is a right, not something that has to be earned. The old duty concept still has sufficient force that increases in leisure time can create tension and a guilt feeling in many people — for example, leisure has

---

*This refers to "production workers," "operatives," etc., in these industries. Total employment in "goods-producing" industries will represent somewhat less than one-third of 1980 employment.

41

to be justified as a necessary reaction to work ("recharging one's batteries") or filled with do-it-yourself projects. Ultimately, a more balanced "gospel of leisure" may be developed, and then we could see a further modification of the "work-as-a-duty" notion. In this regard, the Hippie movement (discounting the extreme, or lunatic, fringe of the movement) may well foreshadow some of the prevalent attitudes twenty-five years from now.

Another perspective on these changing attitudes is provided by an examination of four beliefs that have predominated at various stages of history:

- <u>Work as a necessity:</u> Societies in the early stages of development saw (and still see) work as neither good nor bad. It was simply a prerequisite for survival. As largely agricultural work, its content and rhythm were, for the most part, dictated by forces of nature beyond man's control.

- <u>Work as a social duty:</u> In what can be described as a form of social contract, individuals owed their labors to the tribe or community in return for protection and sustenance.

- <u>Work as a religious duty:</u> The most highly developed form of this belief can be found in the Calvinist doctrine. Work is representative of Man's Fall from Eden; it serves as punishment for sin and prevention for future sinning. The notion that "idle hands make mischief" is one tenet of this belief, along with the conviction that man's labors should be dedicated to the greater glory of God.

- <u>Work as self-actualization:</u> In this view, only now beginning to gain a hold, education, leisure and work are grouped together as steps toward an individual's self-development and improvement.

Only at this last stage is there any possibility of developing a gospel of leisure. In the other stages leisure is thought of as time left over from work, something almost to be apologetic about.

We are not going to see the emergence of a leisure-oriented society overnight or even over the next decade. There is a substantial body of thought that work is as critical and inherent an urge as any biological drive. And, in any case, people will continue to be work-oriented because of their rising economic expectations and need for money. To concede these points, however, should not divert our attention from the fact that the situation is not static, but is changing in some fairly well-defined ways:

42

- There will be a growing, but still tiny, minority drawn from the upper end of the affluence scale who either "drop out" from a sense of alienation or choose the life of the "perpetual student";

- The character of work will be changing markedly, due to advancing technology, shifts in occupational groups (e.g., from manufacturing to services, from blue-collar to white-collar), trends away from hourly pay and time-cards and changes in organizational structure;

- The structure of work will be changing, as work/study programs become more common, sabbaticals are more widely adopted and part-time work accounts for a greater percentage of total hours worked* (perhaps leading to the introduction of modular work-scheduling to enable employees to select the number of modules they want to work);

- People's expectations of the work situation will be higher (and more varied), as a reflection of changing value systems.

The combined effect of these factors must necessarily change, in quite substantial manner, the way people look at work in relation to their lives. And it is this effect that organizations will have to try to assess and factor into their operations.

A more accurate statement than the old work-leisure division could, in the future, be a three- (or four-) way division — work, education/development (sub-divided into "education for one's career" and "education for one's avocation'), leisure or relaxation. In fact, even this probably understates the multiplicity of uses to which "non-work" time will be put.

The potential shifts in attitude might be summed up by saying that tomorrow's blue-collar workers may adopt present-day middle-class work values, while the professional and scientific workers of the future may trend to a less driving, and more avocational attitude to work.

Notwithstanding these changing attitudes toward work, two statistical measures of people's willingness and ability to work will not be significantly changed by 1980. The statistically defined work week (i.e., average weekly hours worked) is expected to continue its

---

*It is not generally recognized that intermittent workers represent one-third of the full labor force; and already one-tenth of hours worked in our economy come from part-time work.

historical decline, but at a somewhat slower rate: at the end of this period it will stand at about thirty-five to thirty-six hours (partly as a result of longer vacations), and the five-day week is expected still to be the norm. The labor market participation rate will hold up and should even edge up a point or two (to around 58 percent) by 1980: while the rate for men will decline slightly (due to longer education and earlier retirement), that for women will rise, with quite dramatic increases recorded for white women in the 35–64 age brackets.

5. GROWING INTERDEPENDENCE OF INSTITUTIONS

Both domestically and internationally, there will be a heightening of the interdependence of institutions — national, state and local; governmental, economic and non-profit. The scope of problems, the speed-up in communications and transportation, patterns of economic activity, population growth and urbanization — all combine to hasten the obsolescence of traditional political, economic and ideological boundaries.

The world is seen as becoming, in Marshall McLuhan's phrase, "a global village." The development of instantaneous, world-wide television will bring national events (and problems) to an international audience, with significant changes in people's thinking about the world as a consequence (as coverage of the Vietnam war has already demonstrated). The internationalization of economic activity will progressively diminish the relevance of national political boundaries (though, as we have already noted, these will persist). As one prominent sociologist noted, "The economy of Venezuela is as much affected by what happens in the Panama Canal as by anything the Venezuelans can do: and the welfare of Jamaican school children is much more affected by the United States and Great Britain than by anything the Jamaican government can do." This trend will be carried a stage further as regional economic groupings are followed by the establishment of political bodies to control them.

Some problems — nuclear power, the population explosion, progress of the developing economies — are, and will be, inherently world problems, however much they may have their roots in national situations. As a result, it will be increasingly hazardous for the United States or any other nation to assume that a narrow definition of "what's best for our country" necessarily represents the best policy decision.

At home, technology and communications have made us a national, not a regional, economy and society. As more and more local problems (e.g., pollution, urban renewal, transportation, education) assume regional and even national importance, there will be a greater meshing of the activities of governments (at all levels), private businesses and non-profit institutions. Thus, a gradual blurring of the traditional divisions between public and private sectors is foreseen, with government intervening in the private sector, but also with private business entering fields traditionally associated with governmental activities.

Economic, technological and social realities are also breaking down the exclusivity of political and ideological dogmas. Thus, we find the Soviet Union prepared to adapt the profit motive, though not the principle of private ownership, to its economic system; while, in the United States, liberals seem more willing to concede a role to private enterprise in the solution of social problems than at any time in the past thirty years. Conversely, there is a growing de facto recognition of the need for an expanding government role, even in capitalist countries, to supply or fund the social services people increasingly demand and to guide the economy by a variety of techniques such as indicative planning,* fiscal and monetary policies, wage-price guidelines. For the future, pragmatism rather than ideological dogmatism is likely to be the major determinant of public policy.

---

*As an example, "le Plan" in France, prepared by the government in cooperation with business "indicates" (as opposed to mandating) medium-term goals in production, investment, employment, etc., and seeks to guide the public and private policies required to achieve them.

6. EMERGENCE OF THE "POST-INDUSTRIAL SOCIETY"

For some two hundred and fifty years, from the founding of James-town to around 1870, the United States existed as an agricultural society. For the next ninety years it became an industrialized society. Now it is on the brink of becoming something different, a form of society that the world has not seen before. Some of the features of this society can be discerned, but lack of precedent dictates caution in predictions: the commonly accepted term, "post-industrial society," is scarcely descriptive of its characteristics, but merely fixes its position on the development time scale.

In one sense, however, the term "post-industrial" does indicate a characteristic of the new form — the relative decline of industry as the prime motive force in our society. To a generation grown up with the notion that industrialization is the hallmark of the U.S.A., such a prospect may seem far-fetched and even alarming. However, a comparison with agriculture may serve to put the future in historical perspective. Agriculture is clearly still a vital force in the United States today — it supplies most of our food and fibers; it accounts for nearly a quarter of our exports; its productivity is exceptional, even by U.S. standards — but no one would, for these reasons, describe this country as an agricultural society. It employs little more than 5 percent of our work force; it is not the source of major innovations in our society; and, above all, it no longer determines our values and way of life.

Something of the same sort of decline — in a modified form and over the long term — faces industry today. In a sense, it will be a victim of its own success. The secondary industries (those that process primary products) have never dominated the employment picture to anything like the extent the primary activities (farming, forestry, fishing, mining) did prior to 1870. From now on, their share of both employment and GNP will be a steadily decling one. In their place will rise the tertiary sector (that supplies services, such as maintenance, transportation and financing, to primary and secondary occupations) and the quaternary sector. Supplying services to tertiary activities and to society as a whole, this latter sector is primarily concentrated in education, the professions (law, medicine, etc.), government and non-profit institutions.

More and more of our national activity will, therefore, take place outside the traditional market economy. This is not, by any means, to say that the private sector as a whole will necessarily diminish in importance: it is, indeed, entirely conceivable that private organizations will perform more of the services and supply more of the systems hitherto supplied by government. However, the growing public-needs market, whether served by private businesses or government (or most likely, a combination of both), differs greatly in structure and operation from the traditional consumer markets that business has served.

Further, there will be a great increase in what Herman Kahn calls "consentives" (as opposed to "marketives") — the great array of non-profit institutions operating in the areas of research, education, health, welfare and the arts. The combination of these forces, coupled with the growing roles of government and education, suggests that profit-making/consumer-oriented operations will decrease as a proportion of the total national effort.

As a result, there are many suggestions to the effect that our traditional economic indicators will have to be broadened to get an adequate measure of our total effort. The case for some form of "social accounting" was made, for instance, in the report of the National Commission on Technology, Automation and Economic Progress (pp. 96–97):

> A system of social accounts, if it could be established, would give us a broader and more balanced reckoning of the meaning of social and economic progress and would move us toward measurement of the utilization of human resources in our society in four areas:
>
> 1. The measurement of social costs and net returns of economic innovations;
>
> 2. The measurement of social ills (e.g., crime, family disruption);

Characteristic of the "Post-Industrial Society"

1. Per capita income about fifty times the pre-industrial.
2. Most "economic" activities are tertiary and quaternary (service-oriented) rather than primary or secondary (production-oriented).
3. Business firms no longer the major source of innovation.
4. There may be more "consentives" (versus "marketives").
5. Effective floor on income and welfare.
6. "Efficiency" no longer primary.
7. Market plays diminished role compared to public sector and "social accounts."
8. Widespread "cybernation."
9. "Small world."
10. Typical "doubling time" between three and thirty years.
11. Learning society.
12. Rapid improvement in educational institutions and techniques.
13. Erosion (in middle class) of work-oriented, achievement-oriented, advancement-oriented values.
14. Erosion of "national interest" values.
15. Sensate, secular, humanist, perhaps self-indulgent criteria become central.

Source: "The Year 2000: A Framework for Speculation on the Next Thirty-Three Years" by Herman Kahn and Anthony J. Wiener (Macmillan, 1967)

3. The creation of "performance budgets" in areas of defined social needs (e.g., housing, education);

4. Indicators of economic opportunity and social mobility.

Such a system of social accounts is regarded as particularly useful in an era when political issues turn less on traditional economic problems and more on those of "social capital." Perhaps most importantly, it would represent a start toward measuring the total impact, rather than just the economic consequences, of public and private programs, and provide, through over-all cost-benefit analyses, a more rational basis for making critical choices.

Insofar as a dominant institution will arise in the new growth sectors (which are, for the most part, characterized by smaller, decentralized units), it is more likely to be the educational institutions (particularly the university) than government. This is because, in the post-industrial society, key importance will attach to innovation and new theoretical knowledge, neither of which will government be well equipped to supply. The university, on the other hand, is by its very nature designed to produce and mobilize innovative knowledge, as the industrial firm was geared to mobilize resources for mass production. Thus, even though educational institutions may not, by themselves, account for a majority of employment, education per se will be the dominant force determining our way of life and value system. It is from this probable development in the new society that an alternative title — the "learning society" — derives.

For the short term, however, campus unrest — whether violent or not — may prove to be a distraction from this broad societal role. There are many signs that, for the next few years, colleges and universities may rather experience a "turning inward" to deal with their own internal problems of student demands, curriculum revision, financing, governmental relationships, etc. As a result the catalytic role that some postulate for universities in the post-industrial society may well not fully develop in this coming decade.

Along with these shifts in the societal power structure comes a range of value system changes such as those hypothesized by Kahn and Wiener in their book, "The Year 2000" (see box, p. 48).* The principal determinants of these changes are the increases in technology, affluence, education and internationalization of so much economic and political activity. The changes themselves may well be, for many people, the most unsettling feature of this "post-industrial society" — more unsettling, for instance, than specific events such as campus riots or the advent of the space age. The perceived threats to what have been considered traditional, immutable values in our culture will thus be fiercely resisted by many, particularly in the lower

_____

*A more comprehensive treatment of probable value system changes is given in Chapter 5.

middle class, in an effort to maintain a core of stable values to cling to in an otherwise changing world. Many of the social tensions of the next decade will have their roots, directly or indirectly, in such struggles over values.

7. PLURALISM AND INDIVIDUALISM

Although the "mass society" (i.e., a national society with a large and growing population) will obviously persist, there will be some reversal of the past thirty years' trend toward centralization and a strengthening of the individual's importance in the social structure. The prime reason for this decentralization of power and action is, of course, the need for flexibility and variety of both response and initiative in dealing with change. Change will be too fast-moving, too pervasive, too varied for it to be dealt with on a centralized monolithic basis.

Already there is a developing recognition that, for instance, the Federal government cannot single-handedly tackle the complex problems of poverty, pollution and urban renewal. This trend is regarded as bringing about a general strengthening and upgrading of local and state governments. While these governments have been growing faster than the Federal government in recent years, their growth has been rooted mainly in expenditures for education. In the future, their growth will be more broadly based, and the caliber of their constitutions, structures and staffing will be upgraded. The event that marked the opportunity for this reform of state governments, and for their assumption of added duties, was the Supreme Court's "one man-one vote" decision: if state governments could be made more representative of their urban population, the urban centers would, hopefully, not have to turn so much to the Federal government for action. The prospect now is that this opportunity will be realized — though slowly, in view of the organizational inertia that characterizes many state administrations and legislatures.

At the local level, two trends are of particular significance in this regard. In view of the growing inter-relatedness of institutions and their problems, there will be some growth of regional (e.g., urban-suburban) authorities or other arrangements to deal with shared problems such as rapid transit and pollution control. This can be viewed either as a centralizing force (relegation of local powers to a "super" agency) or as a decentralizing force (delegation of co-ordinated planning and operations that might otherwise have taken place at the state level). Certainly, it will be a force for pluralism, in multiplying the number and level of governmental agencies.

More pronounced and more clear-cut will be the growing emphasis, within urban governments, on community control. While predominantly associated with the racial struggle, this trend is, in fact, part of a broader movement in search of a more participative form of democracy. The movement is already underway, in a number of cities, over control of local schools and poverty programs; and the signs point to a broadening and acceleration of the trend as it extends to other cities and other types of community services or political organization.

A further decentralizing force in our society is the growth of the tertiary and quaternary sectors of the economy (noted previously), with their multiplicity of small units. In particular, the emergence of non-profit institutions — research, welfare, educational and medical organizations — as a "third force" between government and private business will bring a new dimension of opportunity in employment and an outlet for creative talent and hence provide a new element of competition for talented manpower.

A new wave of individualism is predicted to re-shape many of our social and organization patterns. Members of minority groups and college youth have already set the pace and tone for this trend, with their emphasis on realizing the traditional American goals of equality and individual dignity. And the beginnings of a new and more powerful "feminist" movement are already discernible: many of the minority goals in equal employment opportunity will, for example, be adopted by women. In these and other instances the rallying cries of the cause will be equality; personal worth; resistance to treatment as stereotypes; insistence that individual rights be valued over organizational convenience.

The emergence of such a trend may appear surprising in a mass society. But it is, of course, only a manifestation of the latent drive of every individual to express and realize himself — a drive which has been checked by earlier trends (mass production, large organization, etc.), but which will be reinforced by future trends. In an era in which "human capital" is an organization's most precious resource — and in which a tight labor market persists — no institution can escape the need for a more individualized treatment of its members.

It is a reasonable hypothesis that all types of organization will be operated less and less by the dictates of administrative convenience and more and more to meet the wants and aspirations of their membership. So long as organizations were concerned principally with a relatively stable environment and the maintenance of internal order, they could rely on the routine administration of detailed procedures (the great strength of bureaucratic systems). Dealing with the uncertainty of change reduces the value of set procedures and increases the value of individual initiative.

Education and affluence strengthen the individual's role by improving his "market value," removing most of the fear of unemployment and economic failure and maximizing his mobility and range of employment choices. These factors are viewed as making it highly improbable that individuals (or minority groups — to take a special case) can, in the future, be held in anything like the position of subordination to authoritarian organization that has been the pattern in the past. If the older organizations do not satisfy these demands for individuation, tomorrow's youth will be more inclined, and more able, to establish new, smaller and more meaningful (to them) organizations, and less inclined to "knuckle under."

In fact, the mass society itself reinforces this drive by making a person's individuality his most prized possession. The "post-industrial" society is seen as nurturing greater sensitivity about the pressures for conformity in large organizations, greater willingness

52

and ability to resist these pressures and greater resistance to a threatened invasion of privacy from any source.

8. THE URBAN/MINORITY PROBLEM

Minorities and the cities have a complex of problems in common — poverty, unemployment, welfare, high crime rate, inadequate housing and schooling, segregation. Though some whites share in these problems, and though rural poverty is (by any measure) twice as severe as urban poverty, it is among the minority population in our urban centers that the problems exist in their most visible and complex form.

The urban riots of 1967 provided a "moment of truth" for the American public and generated a real commitment to solution of these problems as a national goal.* Though this is more a matter of backlog of "unfinished business" for society (i.e., bringing a minority up to the present level of achievement and aspirations of the majority) than a new development, there can be little doubt that this problem will be the dominant one on the domestic social, political and economic scene for the next ten years.

The threat of failure is a real one. Any social revolution of these dimensions can easily rip apart the social fabric of a community — or a nation. The danger will lie in a divisiveness that will not merely wreck the consensus of the American center, but split the country into warring camps — the economic "have-nots" versus the "haves"; the political radicals versus the conservatives.

Compared with the situation twenty (or even ten) years ago, present conditions on the minority relations front are very fluid. There is virtually unanimous agreement that changes in this situation are inevitable: it is too volatile and unstable to persist in its present condition for any length of time. Although even close observers of

_____

*One recent social phenomenon has been the apparent willingness of the American public to respond to, and stick with, long-range goals despite their costs and difficulties (e.g., civil rights, despite the riots; Vietnam, despite the cost and protests; space program, despite the cost and early frustrations).

53

this scene profess their inability to make specific predictions —
because they find the future, in many important aspects, so
uncertain — they are in substantial agreement on the nature of
the forces that will shape these developing conditions.

The Youth Effect

One of the more significant forces will be the rising tide of youth,
in both the white and non-white communities, coming on the scene
with new aspirations and new values. A wave of 58 million children
aged five to nineteen — nearly one-third of our total population — was
poised, in 1966, to sweep over our institutions in the Seventies. By
1980 they will be in the age groups 20–34 — more than 21 million
over the number in those age groups in 1966.

The potential effect of this youth wave on social attitudes, institutional action and political programs dealing with the minority problem
will certainly be a force to reckon with — especially if a real generation gap in thinking on this issue does reveal itself and is then translated into action. For the moment, a number of general observations
can be made about the probable impact of our youth:

(a) The younger blacks, who have come of age in a decade of re-
    volt, will clearly be more impatient with the status quo, or
    even with progress, than their elders. There is a sense of
    momentum, and a conviction in the necessity of pushing hard
    for equality, that they are not likely to abandon.

(b) The better educated among white youth will be more likely than
    their parents or their less well-educated peers to be suppor-
    tive of the minority cause. Further, they will fairly rapidly
    get into positions where they can do something about it, working
    on institutional change from the inside.

(c) The children of white blue-collar workers, on the other hand,
    will be far more likely to carry into the Seventies their
    parents' resentment of minority progress and "affirmative
    action" programs. In part, this resentment is born of a feeling
    that "special favors" are not called for or deserved by minori-
    ties; in part, of the presumed competition that will ensue for
    their jobs.

54

The Central City/Suburban Division

In our metropolitan areas, today, resides approximately 70 percent of our total population, both white and non-white. However, one of the most significant indicators of today's urban/minority crisis is that, within these areas, twice as large a percentage of blacks as whites live in central cities, while only slightly more than one-third as many live in suburbs. This phenomena of "black cores, white fringes" in our major cities is the result of extensive minority in-migration and white out-migration during the past twenty-five years; but it is expected to continue to shape the future course of race relations in the Seventies.

Admittedly, a number of new trends are emerging to change the total picture:

(a) In the first place the farm-city migration may be ending; certainly, the crest of the wave has passed.

(b) There is some evidence that the black population in central cities has started to level off, while still increasing in the suburbs. In the two-year period 1966–1968, for instance, blacks actually decreased their central city population by some 300,000 and increased their suburban representation by half a million.

(c) Central cities will account for a declining percentage of our population. As a result of the leveling-off among the black population and a continued out-migration of whites, the suburban-central cities population gap will widen.

However, these factors can only, at best, be said to slow the future worsening of the problems rather than to reverse them. For instance, the spread in growth of the black population, and their migration out of central cities, will mean that the potential problem of racial confrontation will extend to suburbs and other towns that have so far not been directly affected to any extent. Such a movement can also, of course, lead to the creation of new "suburban ghettos" if the segregated housing patterns of the cities are allowed to recur.

A New Mood of Militancy

A developing force for change is the growing spirit of militancy among minority groups. The virtually unanimous expectation is that a recurrence of Detroit-type riots is unlikely; but there is an equally universal prediction that we must anticipate continued outbursts of some sort. The massive outbreaks in Detroit, Newark, Watts and Washington are seen in retrospect as largely self-destructive convulsions of the black ghettos, born of bitterness, alienation and despair.

The outbreaks are not expected to occur again in their past form because they have cost the black community too much in death, destruction and shattered businesses. If violence does develop, the expectation is that the pattern will be one of more calculated and selective attacks rather than of general, indiscriminate uprisings (though these are still possible in cities that have not yet experienced riots).

It would, however, be a blatant misreading of the new mood of militancy to interpret it exclusively in terms of such violence. Violence will be the exception, rather than the rule, in urban/minority relations. The true meaning of the growing militancy will be found in a pervasive activism in pushing, hard and persistently, for rights, representation and economic equality. As such, this militancy will affect communities and institutions of all types and sizes, and so will touch the lives of many more millions than will outright violence.

The Swing from Integration

Partly as a consequence of the slow progress toward school desegregation since the Supreme Court's Brown decision in 1954, integration has lost some of the appeal it had in the "old" civil rights days. For the greater number of minorities, integration still stands as an ultimate goal — certainly as contrasted with the notion of a separate nation — but even here its terms of reference are in process of being re-defined. And other goals, other motivators will be more powerful forces in the Seventies.

For one thing, the new militancy of the minority community is prone to interpret integration as a goal that has been set by whites and toward which progress is controlled by whites. To some, "integration" (in quotation marks) is itself a condescending gesture of white superiority.

Yet the pendulum has not swung over to separatism in its most extreme form. By far the greater number of minorities are likely to continue to argue that America is their homeland and that they will press for their position of equality in it as a matter of right.

Somewhere between old style integration and new style separatism lies a concept that will be a dominant motivator of the future, particularly in the black community. Perhaps best described as an emphasis on "separateness," it will represent something of a voluntary segregation or withdrawal within racial and cultural boundaries for the purpose of strengthening blacks' sense of pride, identity and purpose.

This period of "separateness" seems likely to be a transitional phase, for minority groups to find themselves and gain their own forms of political and economic power, before any possibility of coalescing as equals in society.

The immediate objective, then, is not integration, but equality — and equality in an open, pluralistic society. The two goals are not the same, and the distinction between them should be clearly made. The tactics and the consequences of each are different. For the foreseeable future there is no prospect of a "melting pot" society that obliterates racial and cultural differences: they will have to be recognized (and dealt with) for what they are, not as badges of innate superiority and inferiority.

Power Struggle of the Seventies

Power — economic and political power — will be the dominant criterion by which the minority community will judge the value of public and private programs and the extent of its progress. The main struggle in race relations in the Seventies will not be over integration and legal rights, but about a just and proportionate sharing of power in society. That is what the increasingly popular slogans of "community control," "black power" and "maximum feasible participation" are all about.

The ultimate power that most minorities (like most whites) want is the power to direct the course of their own lives. To achieve this power, they are seeking control of their community institutions, to set their own goals and chart their own course, free of white interference. The struggle has been joined, in a few cities, primarily over control of the local school system and poverty programs. We must expect that it will spread very quickly to many other communities and be extended to other community services (fire, police, hospital, sanitation, recreation) and businesses (banks, supermarkets, credit).

Acquisition of power will become fiercely important to the minority community, both for the control that is gained and as a symbol of progress. Any transfer or sharing of sovereignty within a system is at best a difficult operation; and the fierce urgency of minority demands for power will make the next decade a particularly troublesome one for the present economic and political "Establishment."

A Testing of the American System

It is not unreasonable to assert that the decade of the Seventies will see a new testing of the American system. Just as our political system was tested and adjusted in the 1860's, and our economic system in the 1930's, so our social system will be tested in the 1970's for its ability to provide opportunities for all minorities to move into the mainsteam of economic life.

With nearly 90 percent of the population and close to a monopoly of power, the white community—and, in particular, white leadership—will determine the outcome of this test. Whether there will be progress toward a pluralistic open society or regression into polarized warring camps depends predominantly on the attitudes and actions of this majority. And, since there is no inevitability about the outcome, it becomes clear that leadership decisions—including decisions by business leadership—will have the ultimate determinative effect.

4

CHANGING INSTITUTIONS

The extent and timing of the impact of these developing trends will, obviously, vary from institution to institution: the caliber of the adaptation to, or shaping of, these trends will be even more varied, depending on the awareness, imagination and courage of the particular institution. The extremes of vigorous action and resigned inaction may, of course, divert or hasten the course of a trend and so affect the process of change in the institution itself.

The following example may serve to illustrate this point:

There is a developing consensus of legislative, administrative and public opinion that private enterprise has a part to play in the growing "public needs" sector — an area that, up till now, has been considered a government preserve.

If companies step up to this new opportunity, then they will have to develop new products and services, learn how to operate with new patterns of governmental and community relationships, establish new organization structures and operating procedures. But they will have strengthened the trend to pluralism, arrested a top-heavy centralization of power and an excessive concentration of employment in government (with all that this would imply for employee relations and collective bargaining practices).

If, however, private enterprise does not enter this new arena, then companies may temporarily continue to "do business as usual" but, sooner or later, they will feel the heavier impact of government regulations and taxation. And many predict that there would be an inevitable shift in the power structure in favor of government, and against business, because (it is argued) there would be no alternative then to government's attempting to undertake solutions to all social problems.

The recent impact of trends has been so sharp and severe on a number of institutions, most notably our cities and some universities, that the question has been raised about the inevitability, or even desirability, of a radicalization of our institutions. Originally raised as a rallying cry by a tiny minority which despairs of any progress "within the system," a radical solution to the problems of institutional rigidity has come to be much more widely discussed — and feared.

For a variety of reasons, however, the probability of any radicalization of society in the Seventies is of a very low order. In the first place, there is a strong core of conservatism in the American make-up that tends to make changes evolutionary rather than revolutionary: many issues that are first posed in revolutionary terms get finally resolved in rather pragmatic ways. Secondly, the inability or unwillingness of the radical element to espouse specific, viable alternatives tends to alienate potential supporters who are deterred by the futility of a nihilistic approach. And lastly, perhaps, there is some emerging evidence that some institutions are starting to practice the policies of self-renewal espoused by John W. Gardner.

Having discounted the possibility of radicalization, however, one must not go to the other extreme of supposing that little will change. Indeed, if institutions are to endure in substances, they will have to change greatly in function, style and values. Such changes will be profound and widespread, in all institutions, as a result both of internal pressure from the changing aspirations of their members and of external public, governmental, economic and technological pressures.

Technological change, by itself, will demand a greater degree of institutional change than is generally recognized. There are three sweeping and pervasive institutional changes that technology requires of any organization, and society, if it is to be both fully utilized and adequately controlled:

1. The organization (company, school, government agency, etc.) must encourage experiment, flexibility and variety: this will come about partly as a consequence of higher educational levels, partly through re-structuring the management system of the organization.

2. There must be a thoroughgoing democratization of the system: science and technology, which set in motion a process of continual change, are inhibited by the traditional hierarchical and authoritarian system (but will, in the long run, subvert it), but flourish in (and foster) a climate that is egalitarian, pluralistic and open to dissent.

3. There must be created a capability of seeing technological change as a whole, including the social, political, cultural and psychological side effects: this is a matter of concern both to society as a whole* and to an individual organization.

In specific ways, too, technology will continue to change, at an accelerating rate, the products and services an organization offers, the methods it employs, the skills it requires. This will be as true, for instance, of education and medical services as it is of business and government. For the next decade, computerization will no doubt be the dominant influence; but, by the end of that time, we shall stand on the brink of an even more significant force — the results of

---

*Hence, for instance, the suggestions (already mentioned, p. 47) for a system of "social accounts."

biomedical research that will raise social, legal, political and ethical questions about the nature and purpose of man himself.

One of the major institutional requirements of an era of radical change is the growing importance, in all types of organizations, of formulating explicit goals. As a society, we are not yet, and shall not be within this time span, so affluent that we can afford to do everything at once: we have, in other words, to make choices. Indeed, it can be argued that increasing affluence and technology will enlarge our range of options, by bringing more of man's historical aspirations within the realm of the possible, and so make choices more, not less, difficult and important than in a poorer society in which options are strictly limited.

Establishing goals will be a way of making these choices explicit, whether for the nation or for a company. In this way, informed debate about objectives can take place, and the choices can be made more rationally.

Explicit goals will also be needed to create organizational focus and identity in an era of change. It is, no doubt, true that planning and goal-setting increase in importance as they increase in difficulty. Though the degree of future uncertainty and the number and strength of external forces might appear to make goal-setting an exercise in futility for any organization, it must be attempted if the system is not to lose direction and fall victim to centrifugal forces. A search for meaning, purpose and identity — which we now think of primarily as an individual quest — will become necessary for organizational, and even national, vitality and self-renewal.

1. GOVERNMENT AND POLITICS

The central facts of the current political scene are (a) the dominance of the Federal government (despite recent growth of state and local units) and (b) the transfer of power from legislative to executive branches at every level. The prediction is that in the next ten years there will be some decentralization of power from the national to state and local levels, but a further institutionalization of the Presidency and other executive branches.

62

The Division of Powers

Because foreign policy and demands of the "public needs" sector are likely to be the major determinants of national policy, the crucial issues of this next period are expected to be political rather than economic in nature. And because we are now a national society and polity, these issues and the decisions on them will center on the national government. In this sense there will be a continuing expansion of Federal power and influence. In absolute terms there will be increases in employment and expenditures at the national level.

However, in relative terms, a shift in power and influence back to the state and local governments is foreseen. In part, this shift will stem from the continuing growth in the importance and cost of education (which, despite being a matter of national concern and influence, will continue to be implemented at the state and local levels). In part, it will be a consequence of the practical need to involve every level of government in the solution of social problems (urban renewal, pollution control, poverty, etc.). As was mentioned earlier, there is a growing feeling that the Federal government simply will not be able to cope with these problems on its own: it will not have the resources; and, even if it had them, it would not have the flexibility.

One way of viewing this trend is to see in it a slow but steady shift in the functions of the Federal government from the operation and management of programs to a role of goal-setting, funding, catalyzing and measuring. There will not be, even by the end of the decade, a complete shift away from a "do-it" role, but the changed functional balance will be unmistakable. The space program has demonstrated that even Federally managed programs do not have to be Federally operated. Beyond this, there is a growing recognition that, like an over-centralized company, the nation may, with the present role of the Federal government, end up by having neither well-run programs nor a well-designed set of national goals and priorities.

With both the importance and difficulty of goal and priority setting on the increase, it is predictable that this function should grow in stature at the national level. As it does, it will displace some current operations to other levels of government or other organizations, both business and non-profit — a move toward decentralization that will be in harmony with the basic trends toward pluralism and participation. How such national goals should be formulated, debated and finally selected in a pluralistic society will itself be a political question of the first order in the Seventies. The first step toward institutionalizing this national goal-setting process has already been taken with the establishment of a National Goals Research Staff in the White House.

One consequence of this re-alignment of powers and responsibilities among the various levels of government will be the emergence of a "new Federalism" seeking to develop a system of truly shared powers between governments. With a few exceptions (e.g., foreign policy and defense), all levels of government are expected to be involved in all programs, with no clearly separable roles. Within such a structure, power would be distributed widely and variedly. Thus, the main policy decisions and most of the implementation on the highway program would take place at the state level; in urban renewal, they would be at the city level (though state and Federal governments will give increasing emphasis to urban affairs); in pollution control, the initial effort would be at the Federal level, with progressive dissemination of responsibilities as the program takes hold.

Another aspect of this "new Federalism" would be increasing involvement of business in the implementation and management of government-funded projects. Both sides are realizing their need for each other (business, for the growth markets in the public sector; government, for the management and technical resources of business), and are thus becoming more flexible in their policies of accommodation. From the time of the Civil War till Wilson's Presidency, business had been Hamiltonian in its belief in a strong Federal government. Since then — and particularly since the Thirties — its commitment has been to upholding the rights of state and local governments in the belief that they would be more manageable and more

64

sympathetic to business interests. Recent experience of contractual relationships with the Federal government in the defense, atomic energy and space programs has modified this anti-Federal viewpoint, and — since there is now a real prospect of stronger local government units — the door seems open to a broader, deeper and more effective partnership between government and business than ever before.

To what extent is this sharing of powers likely to be reinforced by a sharing of revenues (along the lines of the plan advanced by the Nixon Administration)? Three points have been emphasized in considerations on revenue-sharing. In the first place, any reallocation of taxing authority is unlikely to materialize, as there is widespread agreement that the Federal government is the most efficient tax collector. Secondly, any "untied" sharing of revenues will have to be preceded by reform of state and local governments (see pp. 50–51). Thirdly, we are so committed to grants-in-aid for the next ten years that it would take an end to the Vietnam war and a de-escalation of defense expenditures to release sufficient additional funds to make revenue-sharing a substantial and worthwhile program.

Whether or not revenue-sharing materializes on a major scale, Federal aid is expected to continue to flow directly to cities, by-passing state governments. Even if constitutionally authorized to raise more funds, cities would be hard pressed to do so because of their poor credit base (a persistent condition), and because — with the Federal income tax rates unlikely to be substantially lowered — they are seen as being already at or near the popularly acceptable ceiling of total tax burden.

As to the other feature of the current political landscape — the growth of executive power at the expense of the legislative bodies — there is unlikely to be a similar reversal of the trend. The institutionalizing of the offices of the President, governors, mayors and town managers is certain to continue as a result of the need for detailed planning and highly technical decisions. In the process, the professional administrators and the technologists in these offices, who will be responsible both for the "alternative futures planning" and for their implementation, will be in a position to enter more and more into the shaping of the political decision-making process.

Future Political Alignments

There is a growing body of evidence that political groupings will become re-aligned along a different axis from that of the past thirty years. At least since the days of the New Deal, the spectrum of political opinion from conservative to liberal has been represented by the range of beliefs about the desirable extent of Federal government involvement in the economic and social life of the country. There are indications that this will no longer be the main axis of American politics, as liberals start to call for a strengthening of government below the Federal level (e.g. community control, stronger urban or metropolitan governments) and conservatives accept some of the principles of economic management (e.g., the use of fiscal and monetary policies as stabilizing forces). This is not to say that there will be no debate on this issue, only that the major debates are likely to be focused on other issues.

What, then, will be the principal basis for political alignment? The race issue is, of course, one possibility — and a virtual certainty if visible progress toward a solution is not made, if riots resume with greater force, if black militancy becomes more widespread. However, if even an uneasy equilibrium can be maintained and the black moderates can be strengthened by evidence of tangible gains (as now, on balance, seems possible), then the race issue per se will more probably mark off splinter parties at the two extremes. And whatever else the real "new politics" may be, it will be the politics of a majority, not of an alienated minority.

The principal debating area for the great middle majority of American politics is more likely to be the nature, and order, of national goals and priorities. This is probable at least at the level of national politics. At the state and local level the dividing issues are more likely to be (1) urban renewal, in its broadest sense; (2) urban-suburban relationships; and (3) taxation/financing, which would tie in with the problem of the ordering of state and local priorities. The issues are, thus, likely to be more complex and shifting than in the past, with the composition of political groupings correspondingly shifting from time to time. Such temporary alignments are likely to lead to an even more pronounced "independent" registration and voting.

We are predictably entering a prolonged period of political ferment and vocal dissent as alliances break up and re-form and as new issues confront the electorate. For, while there may be a "nationalizing" trend that will diminish the depth and harshness of the old divisions (e.g., between North and South, East and West, farm and city), new divisive issues will take their place — racial problems; the control of crime and riots; the consequences of further U.S.-U.S.S.R. detente; the extent of U.S. overseas involvement; issues of productivity/efficiency versus conservation/beautification; debate over the balance between public and private approaches to the solution of social problems. As these new issues come to a head, we may stand in greater danger of polarization of political opinion than at any time in our nation's history except for the Civil War and Depression eras.

Some of the incipient political turmoil was already apparent in the 1968 Presidential election campaign, with its surprising twists and turns, its Chicago convention violence and the serious emergence, for only the third time in this century, of a third party. On each of these three occasions (1912 and 1924 being the other occasions),* the times were marked by intense social conflict, sharp political differences and the failure of the two major parties to adapt adequately to changing times and needs.

For all their differences, the Wallace movement and the "youth crusade" under the banner of Eugene McCarthy were both disenchanted with the political processes of the major parties and wanted government "returned to the people." Looking to the causal trends

---

*1948 scarcely falls in this category because, despite the splits caused by the Henry Wallace and Dixiecrat movements, their combined share of the total popular vote amounted to only 5 percent.

behind these two movements and projecting their development into the next decade, one can hypothesize:

(a) That the projected polarization of political opinion will probably materialize, at least to the extent of the enlargement of political effort at the extremes of the spectrum. The electorate would thus be more tri-modal than in the recent past, with splinter parties (or at least much greater activity) on the right and left and a reduced (but still dominant — say 75–80 percent) middle ground over which the two major parties would contend.

(b) That third parties will, however, be mainly restricted to the local level. Although a strong third party showing in the 1972 Presidential race remains a distinct possibility, splinter parties historically have great difficulty in developing into truly national parties because of their inability to take root at the congressional level.

(c) That the two major parties will have to adapt their procedures and policies to deal with these challenges from the extremes. Specifically, they will reduce the power of the old-line "bosses" and party professionals by acceding to the demands for wider participation and greater democratization of internal processes (witness, the proposed joint Democratic-Republican study aimed at revising convention procedures).

(d) That the South will be lost to the Democrats as an effective political force. In 1968 Humphrey polled under 30 percent in the eleven Southern states, continuing the Democratic slide that set in during the 1948 campaign. In congressional voting on issues of major national importance, Southern representatives and senators seem certain to continue their conservative/ Republican alliance. This element of the "New Deal" coalition seems likely to be missing from any re-alignment of the Democratic party. Only the pull of seniority and committee chairmanships will keep these congressmen nominally within Democratic ranks. If the Democrats lose control of Congress for any length of time, the Southern trend to an overt Republican allegiance would be considerably hastened.

(e) That reformist youth will not have the political weight sometimes ascribed to it. Even in 1985 the median age of voters will be 40–41 (or 39, if — as seems likely — the voting age is reduced to 18). Political parties will make special efforts to court the youth vote, and young persons and ideas will have greater influence on political thinking and processes. But political arithmetic will inevitably moderate the extent of change, particularly on issues involving expenditures and taxation.

The political history of this country, after its opening essentially "non-partisan" phase, can be divided roughly into three major periods

— from Jefferson through Jackson; from Lincoln through Hoover; from Roosevelt through Lyndon Johnson* — each dominated by one of the major parties, though with significant interruptions by the other party. The latest process of political re-alignment is still in such a formative stage that it is not yet possible to say whether the Nixon Presidency is ushering in a fourth period, or merely another interruption in a continuing Democratic regime. Certainly there is no inevitability about the eclipse of either party: factors will be working for and against each. Major elements of the Democratic coalition — labor, blacks, intellectuals, Jews — held together well at all levels in 1968: but the Republicans stand to gain from the population movement toward the West away from the Northeast, the Democrats' stronghold. The issue may be determined both by the speed and extent of party reform and by the positions taken on the ordering of our national priorities.

2. THE ECONOMY

The major structural changes that are likely to take place in the economy in the next decade have already been mentioned in previous sections and need only be summarized here:

- The relative decline of the goods-producing sectors of the economy;

- The growth of the services, trade and finance sectors;

- An increase in the number and importance of non-profit institutions and "Comsat-type" organizations;

- More conscious intervention of government policy and planning;

- A further flattening of the business cycle.

By 1980 a trillion and a quarter dollar economy is predicted, some of whose general dimensions are indicated in the following table:

The Economy in 1980

Total population (millions)	228
Labor force participation rate	58.3%
Civilian labor force (millions)	97.9
Unemployment rate (% of labor force)	4.0%
Gross National Product (1965 $, billions)	1,250
Per capita GNP (1965 $)	5,480
Median income per family (1965 $)	10,450

*The period between Jackson and Lincoln was highly fragmented, with no clear political domination by any party.

Clearly a key factor in charting the course of economic progress is a projection of the rate of productivity improvement. On this point, majority opinion places the average annual productivity increase somewhat above 3 percent, though the extremes ranged from a low of 2.5 percent to a high of 4.0 percent. Although a case can be made for an improvement rate below that of the post-World War II period (due to lower productivity of women, less experienced workers and the services industries — all factors in the ascendant), the higher rate is predicated on the future pay-off from the "research explosion," continued high contributions from education and improvements in the productivity of salaried personnel. Combined with a net increase of approximately 1.2 percent a year in labor input, this could produce an over-all annual growth rate of 4—4.5 percent.

The price of the predicted lower unemployment rate (see p. 36) and much tighter labor markets will be a higher rate of inflation than has obtained for the past ten years — up to 3 percent a year (with a fifty-fifty chance of going above that level some years). Labor costs, in particular, will depart from the lower rates of the early Sixties, as unions take advantage of a seller's market, and employers bid up the going rate in competition with each other for skilled manpower. If a 3 percent rate of inflation does persist, 4 (and even 5) percent* settlements could become things of the past, since employees' "rising expectations" have a built-in momentum.

On the price side, public, political and competitive pressures are expected to work to hold increases down. This could cause a more or less permanent return to the profit squeeze. A resumption of the wage-price guideposts, in some form, is generally predicted, but only with the modest expectation that they may help preserve

---

*In 1969, with a 6 percent rate of inflation, settlements were more nearly in the 7 to 9 percent range.

some order in the upward movement and reduce the possibility of "blockbuster" increases. Despite the relative ineffectiveness of guideposts in the past, they are considered to be more likely to be employed again in the future as a technique of government intervention than some alternative weapons in the government's armory — wage-price controls; prenotification of price increases; centralized negotiations or tax rewards for restraint. Though governmental "jawbone techniques" may well be resumed against key companies and industries, competition is likely to prove the more effective countervailing force. Technology, new products, increases in consumers' discretionary purchasing power and pressure from overseas firms (intensified as the Kennedy Round tariff cuts make their full impact) will all place severe restraints on upward price movements.

Profits will, as suggested, be squeezed in these wage-price pincers: but they would be more stable if the business cycle flattens, as predicted. We may, thus, anticipate public argument that business should be content with a lower rate of return, since much of the cyclical risk will have been removed (so high profits need not be earned in boom times to compensate for low profits or losses in recessions). However, developing technology and foreign competition will demand a rising level of capital expenditures — a trend which will be accentuated by inflated and less variable wage-salary costs, causing management to consider the desirability of a different capital-labor ratio.

If profits are squeezed and interest rates are high (perhaps 6–8 percent, due to inflation and a world-wide capital shortage), how will this increased volume of capital investment be financed? Professor Dean Ammer of Northeastern University suggests that there may be a reversal of the traditional 60–40 split between equity and debt in the financing of assets. If companies want to earn 12–15 percent (after taxes) on equity capital for share owners, and interest rates are 6–8 percent (deductible as an expense), "obviously, it is possible for such a firm to boost its return on equity by relying on debt financing for a greater share of its capital." Further, the flattening of the business cycle will diminish manufacturers' traditional reluctance to shoulder a substantial burden of debt and make them behave more like utilities in this respect.

3. THE LABOR FORCE

Between 1965 and 1975, this country will experience the largest increase in its labor force for any ten-year period in our history — a gain of 20 percent, or 15 million. This phenomenon — caused by the "coming of age" of the post-World War II baby crop — will mean that the labor force will be heavily weighted by younger, better educated but less experienced workers.

The over-all increase will be the net effect of some significantly divergent trends in particular age groups and categories (see table).

Labor Force Change in the United States

Percent Increase 1965-75   By Age, Sex and Color

	Total			White vs.			Nonwhite		
Age	Total	Male	Female	Total	Male	Female	Total	Male	Female
Total	19.5%	16.6%	25.2%	18.7%	15.5%	25.2%	25.9%	26.5%	25.2%
14-19	23.9	21.7	27.2	20.2	18.6	22.6	54.1	45.7	69.6
20-24	41.9	40.6	44.1	40.6	39.3	42.9	50.7	50.0	51.9
25-34	40.7	40.5	41.2	40.8	39.6	44.0	39.8	47.6	28.1
35-44	−5.5	−7.0	−2.5	−6.0	−8.6	−2.1	−1.3	1.4	− 4.9
45-54	12.6	6.7	22.9	12.0	6.1	22.7	17.5	12.4	24.4
55-64	21.9	15.2	34.5	21.9	14.9	35.6	21.4	18.1	26.4
65+	3.8	−2.1	23.5	6.5	−2.1	25.4	1.5	−1.7	7.7

Source: "The Emerging Labor Force of the United States," by Dr. Seymour L. Wolfbein, Temple University (paper prepared for U.S. Chamber of Commerce Council on Trends and Perspective)

For instance:

- There will be double the average increase in young workers (20-24 and 25-34 age groups);

- There will be an actual decline in the 35-44 age group (and a below average gain among the 45-54's);

- Women workers will increase in numbers half again as fast as men, mostly in the over-45 groups;

- Non-white workers will increase in numbers nearly half again as fast as whites, with particular emphasis in the teenage and young twenties groups (which will experience better than 50% gains).

The educational qualifications (and consequent work expectations) of the whole work force will undergo a dramatic upgrading as the 65-year-old worker with an eighth or ninth grade education is replaced by a youth with a high school diploma and, maybe, some college experience. The "generation gap" in education is apparent in the following table:

Median Years of School Completed (1966)

```
18-24 year olds      - 12.5 years school
55-65 year olds      - 10.4 years school
65+    year olds     -  9.1 years school
```

By 1975, six out of ten workers over 25 will be high school graduates, and one out of four will have had some college education.

The employment categories of the 1975 labor force have been highlighted earlier — the continuing shifts toward services occupations, and toward white-collar jobs. By 1975 the services categories will account for about two-thirds of non-agricultural employment, while manufacturing will slip to around 25 percent (versus 28 percent in 1965). Within the services categories a major difference of opinion exists regarding the trend in government employment — with Dr. Seymour Wolfbein of Temple University projecting a 39 percent increase in numbers; Professor Robert Turner, of Indiana University, a 20 percent increase; and the Hudson Institute, only a 12 percent increase. (These figures imply, respectively, an increase in government employment to 17.6 percent of total employment; a leveling off around 14 percent and a decline to 13 percent.) These differences presumably reflect, in part, differing assumptions about the extent to which private enterprise will intervene in the public sector (either directly or on government contract). Interestingly, however, only one of the projections (Wolfbein's) results in a relative increase in government employment as a percent of the labor force.

In one sense, the discussion about which projection will prove correct is an academic one, as a glance at the Post Office situation will make clear. It is a reasonable assumption that out of the current congressional debate about the re-organization of the Post Office will come some different form of corporate structure. But it is also reasonable to predict that (except for statistical purposes) the new entity, with its three-quarter of a million employees, will not be clearly a government unit (as the present Post Office is), nor clearly private (as U.S. Steel is), but rather in that intermediate zone where there is (as has been noted) a blurring of the public-private division. Statistically, however, the classification of this single block of employees materially affects the balance between public and private employment.

Whatever projection is used in this area, the weighting on the side of state and local government employment is clear: Wolfbein, for instance, projects a 48 percent increase for these units of government (versus a 39 percent increase for government as a whole). And at the state and local level the increase will not come, as in the past decade, mainly in elementary and secondary schools (indeed, in line with lower birth rate projections, these schools will show below average gains), but will be concentrated in the areas of higher education, housing and community development, sanitation and pollution control.

The year 1956 was a watershed in economic history, for it was then that white-collar workers (professional, managerial, clerical and sales personnel) for the first time outnumbered blue-collar workers (craftsmen, semi-skilled operatives and laborers). By 1975 they will have widened the gap to nearly a three-to-two ratio:

Occupational Distribution of Civilian Employment: 1975

White collar	48%
Blue collar	34
Service	14
Farm	4

Before 1975 another milestone will have passed when professional and technical personnel — by far the fastest growing segment of the labor force — outnumber skilled craftsmen. As recently as 1947 there were twice as many craftsmen as professional and technical personnel; but by 1975 the professions will be ahead (14.5 versus 13.0 percent of the employed labor force).

If economic predictions come true, unemployment problems of the future will be largely structural, institutional and frictional rather than those caused by deficient demand. These problems will be easier to get at in a rising, relatively stable economy; however, increased demand alone will not solve them. We have seen, for instance, that even an employment rate as high as 96.5 percent will not automatically absorb the hard-core unemployed into the labor force. The hard-core problem of the future will yield only to a concerted effort by business, government and educational institutions to remove the barriers of education, training, movitation, job structure, etc. These efforts can be guided by our prior experience in putting the inexperienced to work in Work War II and in employing the blind and handicapped.

74

Some reference has already been made (p. 44) to projected labor market participation rates and to the average work week. Three additional points might be made in regard to these factors:

(a) The higher participation rate for women is predicated on the probable increase in the attractiveness (and availability) of part-time and intermittent work;

(b) Since 1961 the average work week has been virtually constant, because the historical downward trend has been offset by the cyclical rise during a boom period. The historic trend will reassert itself from now on, but probably at a slower rate due to "moonlighting" and the changing composition of the labor force (managerial, professional and technical workers will tend to work longer hours than blue-collar workers);

(c) The differences in average work week among industries (e.g., in 1965, manufacturing - 41.1 hours versus retail trade - 36.6 hours) are likely to be progressively narrowed during the period ahead (and eventually eliminated, for all purposes, by the end of the century).

4. BUSINESS

The key problem of the next decade for business has been identified as environmental adjustment, at home (e.g., the "post-industrial" shifts in the domestic power structure) and abroad (the fit of the United States in world society and economy). In this process the Board of Directors, with its ability to face both inwards to the firm and outwards to society, can play a crucial role; but, increasingly, every manager will have to adopt this outward- as well as inward-facing posture. If we consider the question, "What topics are appropriate for managerial concern and thought?" it beomes apparent that there will be very few social, political and economic issues inherently excluded from a company president's thinking; and a comparable breadth of outlook will be needed, more and more, farther down the managerial ladder.

Increasingly, business will have to develop "an instinct for survival in a political world," and its managers will need to become more involved in the problem-solving process in governmental and community affairs. Conceivably, companies might find it desirable and necessary to permit managers to devote some percentage of company time to service on public boards or in community activities.

In keeping with the higher aspirations of society in general, business has been reminded that the public will expect more with respect to the "quality of life" in business organizations and the quality of business contributions (in the practical, not the philanthropic, sense) to society. This popular pressure on corporate performance will manifest itself in many ways — for instance:

- In concern for the continuing education and development of employees;

- In quality expectations of products (e.g., the safety and design features);

- In insistence that business pay more of the social cost of problems it has helped create (air pollution, water pollution, traffic);

- In expectation that companies should make, and abide by, long-range goals (that are in harmony with national goals) — particularly if economic fluctuations are going to be moderated;

- In questions about the validity of efficiency as the sole criterion for economic action and over the social (and economic) justification for "conglomerateness."

Reinforcing these popular expectations will be the regulatory and enforcement powers of government. In the years immediately ahead we have been told to expect significant increases in government regulation or pressure on businesses, e.g.:

- In consumer protection, starting with existing legislation on "truth in lending," and extending to packaging and advertising, the quality, safety and maybe even social utility of products;

- In plant location, to encourage (or compel) business to locate establishments in urban or rural development areas, and to control land usage and pollution problems;

- In further concern about corporate hiring, training and testing practices, to support national manpower policies;

- In more strict (but, hopefully, more predictable) prohibition of mergers by large companies.

The criteria by which business performance will be judged in the public mind will be considerably different from, and more sophisticated than, those used in the "muckraking" period — and harder to satisfy than those used by the public when mass production and distribution of consumer goods, or defense contributions, were the prime consideration. In short, the public is implicitly re-writing its "charter of expectations" of companies.

One of these revised expectations is that private companies will involve themselves in the social needs markets. This topic has been brought up repeatedly in the course of this report, and little needs to be added to it here. However, it is worth re-stating the importance (and high hopes) attached to the need for developing what one educator termed "a United States alternative to socialism" in its handling of social problems. The defense and space programs have shown us the way to harness business capability and government funding in the supplying of public needs; and the NASA/AEC model — rather than Comsat, which was shaped by special monopoly and international considerations — could be the pattern for the future. Such an arrangement has the very considerable attraction of making many critical business and technical decisions less influenced by purely political considerations and of multiplying the number of points at which innovative solutions can be introduced into the system. Operating under such arrangements will not, of course, be without problems and dangers for companies (see pp. 59–60), but the strong feeling is that their interests (and society's) will be better served in this way than by compelling government, through business default, to move into every corner of the social welfare market.

It will not be only, or even perhaps mainly, through supplying products that business will make its most useful contribution in this arena. Quite as great a potential — both in scope and in social utility — will be found in the "software" areas, e.g., in supplying management capability, operating education and training programs, employment counseling, providing advice on management/organization.

Partly due to its entry into new fields of endeavor, partly in order to cope with change and the need for rapid and continuous innovation and partly to satisfy the work-aspirations of tomorrow's employees, business will experiment with new organizational forms that will be less

77

structured and hierarchical than traditional bureaucratic systems, more characterized by openness of communications, fluidity and flexibility. In organization, more and more use of the project (or task force) approach is foreseen as a means of keeping abreast of shifting assignments. In managerial style, the new mode will tend toward greater participation and consultation in the decision-making process, since specialization of knowledge is inherently a counter-factor to the absolute authority of the manager.

The task of managing will also become a much more flexible, less structured type of assignment, shifting from day to day, almost from moment to moment. Some areas of business (e.g., consumer goods production) may possess relatively greater stability of organization and management than others (such as project-type operations). But even here shifting consumer demands, constant innovation and more extensive use of numerical control machines will keep production in a constant state of flux. If that is so, then the manager of tomorrow will need to possess much greater flexibility and freedom of action than he does today.

As in government, so in business, more of the effective decision-making probably will be made by the professional and technical experts, the so-called corporate "technostructure" — a term fore-shadowed by Thorstein Veblen with his "soviet of technicians," and by James Burnham's management revolution. These are the specialists who, collectively, will marshal the advanced knowledge and expertise that will effectively influence (if not determine) the main course of corporate decisions.

Compounding the problems of a continually changing organization will be the greater mobility of managerial, professional and technical personnel. In a fluid organization setting, and in an economy of tight labor markets and expanding employment opportunities, it will become progressively easier for an individual to consider his prime commitment to be to his profession and/or his self-development than to a single organization. Predictably, therefore, a key problem will be that of motivating individual commitment to organizational goals. Predictably, too, however successful an organization may be in this regard, it will also (in a sense) fail, for the turnover of this type of personnel is almost certain to increase, even under the best of circumstances.

Part of a company's bid for talented manpower will be through higher compensation and improved benefits programs (see Appendix C for some possible trends). However, with the diminishing marginal utility of income (due to increasing affluence and the "generation gap" in attitudes toward money) will come increasing emphasis on assignments that involve (a) autonomy, (b) creativity and (c) work that is gratifying per se. As changing conditions make obsolete the "tit for tat" theory of compensation ("If you do this, I'll give you that"), work challenges, in a very real sense, will be considered as key elements in the compensation package. Opportunities for education and self-development will also be institutionalized to a point that they are a substantial part of the job offer.

5. UNIONS

In the short run, unions are likely to enjoy a substantial spurt in membership, but to be, in the long run, a declining economic force in our society. However, as with the farm bloc, this declining economic position probably will not significantly diminish their political influence in the 10-year period under consideration. Then, too, over-all trends may well mask counter-trends in particular sectors of the economy; for instance, while unions may decline in importance in the total economy, they may increase in importance in specific industries and occupations.

The numerical growth will come, as is already apparent, from unions' belated entry into the white-collar field via the unionization of public employees. Spurred by President Kennedy's Executive Order and by the passage of state laws permitting collective bargaining with public employees, unions such as the American Federation of Teachers and the American Federation of State, County and Municipal Workers have grown so fast that the "numbers change before the ink is dry on the membership ledger." Furthermore, by removing the stigma of white-collar unionization, the example of such union organizing successes may spur comparable developments in private industry — particularly if teachers' unionization conveys to children (who are, after all, tomorrow's workers) the notion that this is a socially acceptable course of action for white-collar (particularly professional) personnel.

However, the fact remains that the unions within the industrial system — defined here simply as "manufacturing" — representing approximately 45 percent of total union membership will share in that system's relative decline in the economy. Second, the organizing prospects are not so favorable for unions in the many small service firms, among women workers, in the individualized professions and in higher education; and all these are major growth areas in the labor force. Finally, even in the public area, the outlook is not unclouded. Even the most optimistic (for unions) forecast projects public employment only at 17.6 percent of total employment (p. 73); and unions will not conceivably be able to approach anything like a 100 percent organizing effectiveness among these workers. Adverse public reaction to unions' efforts in this area is also likely to develop from two sources:

(a) In the government area, public and union interests are in sharpest conflict over the right to strike;

(b) In this area, particularly at the community level, the cost of union-won salary increases shows up most quickly — in higher taxes.

The net effect of all these developments will probably be to raise union membership temporarily to a slightly higher percentage of the labor force, from which point a new decline will set in.

Union problems will also arise from their image as a self-interest group; from their disconnection from the intellectual community; from leadership difficulties; from problems in managing their own members, particularly the younger ones; and from a developing conflict between white and non-white workers.

No longer do unions enjoy a public image of a crusading spirit of "justice against evil." They are, and will continue to be, seen as just one more self-interest group, concerned (legitmately) with winning "more for their members"; but, increasingly, they are not regarded as entitled to a special measure of public sympathy. Indeed, it is precisely this concern for self-interest that is likely to arouse public retaliation, when this self-interest expresses itself in strikes that hurt the public more than management or in large wage and salary gains that are visibly and directly translated into higher prices (or taxes). This new image has, in the case of some unions (e.g., railroad, newspaper) proceeded so far that the public already considers that the "conservative" and "liberal" roles of management and unions have been switched.

It is the facts behind the new image, too, that have led to the large-scale abandonment of the labor movement by intellectuals, who no longer feel "at home" or wanted in union organizations. This disconnection from the intellectual community is expected to hurt the unions badly in future, when new ideas — quite as much as new leadership — will be required. And a similar dearth of good leadership is predicted, in near-crisis proportions, for the near future. The internal political climate of unions, in which a potential successor will nearly always be viewed as a rival to the present leadership, has not been conducive to executive development programs. And this shortage of leaders will be made even worse in the future as companies, in their intense search for talent to fill the "management gap" (caused by the coming decline in the 35–44 age group), search for leadership potential among union members. Given a choice between a foreman's and a shop steward's position, the chances are that the typical union member will elect to climb the management ladder.

The future supply of both ideas and leadership can be expected to be better in white-collar unions, but is most unlikely to benefit the labor movement in general (and the industrial unions, in particular). Indeed, the exclusivity of white-collar unions is more apt to lead to a hoarding than a sharing of talent. These unions are more likely to develop along the lines of craft unions (exclusive; with emphasis on "authority of knowledge (skill)" and on jurisdictional boundaries) than of industrial unions (inclusive; with emphasis on numbers and lower skills). This could easily lead to a split within (or from) the AFL-CIO by the white-collar members.

A further leadership problem is caused by the growing gap — in aims, aspirations and understanding — between the older national leaders and the younger local members. The younger unionists, whom population trends mark out for a growing role, will tend to be better educated, more middle-class in orientation, influenced by the same forces as their suburban neighbors. In their pluralistic and increasingly leisure-oriented world, the union will play a steadily less important part. Their relationship with the union will be largely professional and business-like, not emotional. One labor editor describes the trend in these words:

> This man does not regard his union as a mother-figure of protection against exploitation and the ruthlessness of management. He looks upon his union as a professional association, much as General Electric looks upon NAM. The union is a more or less efficient way to handle day-to-day dealings with employers — a device for handling specific problems on a generalized, fairly low-overhead basis. He gives the union his power-of-attorney to handle these workaday matters, leaving him almost entirely free from union influence in such areas as politics.

The rank and file dissatisfaction (which has already been revealed in wildcat strikes, rejected agreements and the ouster of leaders) is a measure of this gap in aspirations and career-objectives. Like the managers of other institutions, union leaders face the problems of waning commitment, demands for decentralization and challenges to their authority. Like other managers, too, union leaders are finding a growing restiveness among their employees, for example, among the union organizing agents who are themselves organizing to deal with their union employers.

The stage is thus set for a race between unions and employers (public as well as private) to determine who can first win the commitment of the "new workers." The commitment to one organization or the other will probably never be total; but it can be decisive for the future growth and vitality of that organization.

One final problem confronting unions falls in the civil rights area. Notwithstanding official policy declarations, past support for the civil rights movement has been shaken now that employment, training and promotion questions have become central to the minority cause. To a large degree, the skilled trades versus production workers dispute is polarizing on a whites-non-whites axis, while union opposition to changing membership requirements to open up new employment opportunities to minority groups is becoming a classic struggle between the "ins" and the "outs." Much of the current civil rights leadership is anti-Establishment; and unions, as part of the Establishment, will come into increasing conflict with this new minority militancy.

Many of the recent crises in the public employment sector have centered on, or been tinged with, racial considerations — the New York City teachers' strike and the battle over community control; the issue of union representation in Charleston, South Carolina, hospitals; the Chicago and Pittsburgh controversies over minority employment in construction unions, particularly on public projects. As minority representation in traditionally unionized sectors increases, more and more black employee federations will most likely be set up in opposition to established white leadership in unions. In the resulting struggle, management all too frequently will be caught in the middle, trying to balance its promotion of minority employment opportunities against the need to maintain orderly production.

In terms of organization structure, the prospects are for some decentralization within unions and for "departmentalization" within the labor movement. As to the first, rank-and-file demands for a greater say in determination of union policies are likely to be met by granting some further degree of autonomy in the handling of local grievances and by involving local representatives in joint study groups and in central bargaining teams.

On the other hand, a counter-trend will develop as the scope of bargaining is increased by the use of co-ordinated bargaining* among

---

*Regardless of the prospects for coalition bargaining — and there is considerable disagreement among authorities as to whether or not coalitions will survive natural union divisiveness and legal tests — a greater degree of co-ordination among unions, e.g., in preparations for bargaining, is generally anticipated.

unions and by the extension of local into national bargaining to match a similar development in marketing (as has already developed in trucking, baking and retail food). Larger units will also come into being as the result of mergers between unions, more notably among industrial than craft unions.

These centralizing and de-centralizing forces could lead to some fragmenting of the AFL-CIO federation (an event which could be hastened if a weak man succeeds George Meany) and make the already powerful departments — such as Metal Trades, Industrial Unions, Maritime Trades — the real powers of American unionism. Such a development is all the more probable in view of the likelihood of an eventual breakaway of the white-collar unions from the old-line unions, either into a separate federation or into independent associations or unions.

In an effort to make up for their declining share of the labor force, some unions will turn to greater political and community involvement, particularly in the core cities. This will constitute a new dimension of "political unionism." One goal in this field will be the organization of the poor, both as a means of sharing in the growing political power of the poor and popular appeal of anti-poverty programs, and to build up a reservoir of potential new members as the unemployed poor are gradually absorbed into the work force. On a broader front, we should expect that unions' political activities will turn to espousal of the popular causes of the Seventies — welfare reform, health insurance, pollution control and the like.

6. LABOR-MANAGEMENT RELATIONS

To a very large extent the traditional area of labor-management relations within a company has been institutionalized. Routines, policies, relationships and strategies have been established. Competent and imaginative management will be required to keep these established practices operating and attuned to current business and environmental conditions; but the real payoff will come in the future from mastery of the new problem areas in employee relations, e.g.:

84

(a) The motivation and development of the "new work force" (mentioned in several earlier passages);

(b) The community relations nature of many employment problems: companies will have to learn how to deal relatively more with civil rights and community organizations (which will be leading from strength), as they have dealt with traditional unions.

(c) The emergence of a much greater variety of "employee power structures": companies will have to learn how to handle the essential heterogeneity of employees (largely suppressed till now by "blanket" programs and agreements), which will find expression in new "combinations of interests" (not necessarily unions in the traditional sense) and put an end to the neat bargaining patterns of the past.

In tackling all these new problems — as well as the future versions of old ones — management will have to preserve flexibility of action, which will become so essential to the growth and survival of any organization in a period of change such as lies ahead. Divested of the emotional slogan, "management rights," this becomes the simple organizational necessity for modernizing equipment and processes, instituting changes in job assignments, introducing new products or entering new markets. In seeking to preserve this needed flexibility, however, we are told that management will have (a) to pay careful attention to individual employees' wants and aspirations and (b) be prepared to trade some further measures of job and income security.

Because of the growing complexity and constant change in industrial relations problems, more frequent use of joint study groups and "continuous bargaining" is anticipated.* Since new problems, requiring labor-management resolution, will be arising every day, there will be little to gain — and much to lose — by allowing them to accumulate for resolution in the crisis atmosphere of new contract negotiations once every year or few years. The accumulation of problems would also get worse if the trend to long-term contracts continues, as seems likely. Indeed, the complexity of contract agreements and the highly technical, long-term nature of many benefit programs will make contracts of longer duration increasingly more attractive to

_____

*Already, there are more than 1,200 instances of this practice.

the negotiating parties — if there is some mechanism to take care of new problems arising during the lifetime of the contract.

If any form of continuous study group is to succeed, however, it must be reconciled, on the union side, with the growing demands for membership control in the decision-making process. One reason for the failure of the steel industry's Human Relations Committee was the strong feeling on the part of local members that they were being excluded from participation in decisions arrived at "in camera." For the future, then, the union rank and file will have to be kept involved and adequately informed (without impairing the atmosphere of free discussion within the study group).

With a higher rate of inflation (and, in particular, wage-salary inflation) in prospect, there will be mounting pressure on the Federal government to intervene in the collective bargaining process in an effort to dictate the national interest in price stability. Even though the Nixon Administration has discarded the wage-price guideposts concept, and is philosophically opposed both to controls and to direct intervention, economic and political realities have already compelled it to resort to variations of the "jawbone technique" and to Cabinet-level intervention in the problems of the construction and railroad industries. In the "new economy" of the Seventies it will take only a slight swing in political philosophy, or an increase in the rate of inflation, to cause a return to more free-swinging interventionist policies.

The extent and frequency of government intervention has no inevitability about it: it will be determined, rather, by the degree to which the parties recognize, in their bargaining positions, the twin facts of the increasing interdependence of our economic institutions and the lower frustration tolerance of the public. The prediction is that demands (by either side) that are seen by the public as impairing the balance of equities in a company (or industry or the economy) or imposing hardship on the public will be met with quick resort to governmental action — initially, on an ad hoc basis, but if the "violations" persist, on a sweeping basis.

Another governmental influence in the collective bargaining process, however, will be more certain — the impact that government, as a large employer, will have on developing trends in compensation, benefits and employment practices. With government employment still expanding, and unionization growing fastest in this sector, governments will find themselves more and more drawn into labor-management negotiations. Granted that government is not as monolithic as is sometimes suggested (being made up of units at many levels), settlement terms will rapidly become patterns in this sector, and then — because the sector is highly visible — in the economy as a whole, when a certain level of expectations has been developed.

Government is notoriously a "soft" bargainer (since unions can always resort to political pressure, if they are thwarted at the bargaining table), so the tendency toward inflationary settlements is apt to be greatest in this area. This will make it even more important for business managers to take the leadership in establishing new compensation and employment policies that are sound economically. If they do not, they will have to follow the less desirable, less flexible and more costly practices that are predictable for the public sector.

Considerable uncertainty exists about the prospects for the incidence of strikes in the next decade. Certainly, one can identify a number of forces that might seem to point toward a declining use of the strike, e.g.:

- With increasing automation and decreasing direct labor inputs, several industries (e.g., utilities, telephone, oil refining) are virtually "strikeproof." As this condition spreads, unions will find the strike a progressively less useful weapon.

- Some management opinion (e.g., in airlines, railroad and maritime industries) is in favor of outlawing the right to strike (generally, because they consider themselves to be in a weak bargaining position and believe that they can win a better deal through compulsory arbitration or some other form of third-party intervention). Most management opinion would, however, take a contrary position.

- The public is becoming less and less tolerant of any strike impacting on its convenience.

- Governments are insisting (with public approval) that the new unions with whom they have to deal include in their contracts the "no strike" provisions that have governed, for instance, police forces in the past.

However, the greater probability is that other, countervailing forces will predominate, with a resultant increase in labor-management turmoil. Foremost among these unsettling forces will be the new aspirations of employees, a force compounded of high economic expectations, greater impatience, demands for participation and heightened economic freedom and mobility. Established thinking and procedures in both labor and management will be disrupted by these trends, thus making it harder to reach agreement on settlements acceptable to both parties and to aggressive employee groups.

In the public sector, too, the prospect is not a happy one. Manifestly, "no strike" provisions are being more honored in the breach than in their observance; and there is little reason to anticipate a more tranquil climate until public employers are more adept in their handling of labor-management relations. In some ways, the Seventies in public employee relations may well be analogous to the turmoil of developing labor-management relations in industry during the Thirties. Not until greater competence and more established procedures have been established, and the main unionization surge has abated, will there be any substantial chance of public employment tranquility.

7. EDUCATIONAL INSTITUTIONS

It has been said that it takes thirty years for a new idea to permeate through our educational system; that schools cause children to "grow up absurd"; that universities are "museums." Yet universities are responsible for developing much of society's new knowledge and basic research; and they are predicted, ultimately, to play a dynamic role in changing society in the future.

The contrast between the educational system's ability to generate innovation for other institutions and its inability to absorb innovation into its own bloodstream is marked. Hopefully, this will diminish as the new generation of young teachers takes over. Out of the developing ferment on the campuses, in regional research centers and corporations' ventures into the field will come new approaches to organization, methodology and materials, e.g.:

- As in business, there will be an approach toward individualization. This will involve a radical departure from the traditional "lock-step" progress through the schools and a revision of the "grade-level expectations" that are so much a part of our present culture. Increasing emphasis will be placed on having every child proceed at his own pace through the learning process.

- Partly as a consequence of this development, there will be movement toward greater flexibility in scheduling a school time and in class size. The self-contained classroom is on its way out, to be replaced by a "mix" of large-class sessions, small group discussions and individual learning and by departmentalization and team teaching.

- The "new math" and "new science" are merely precursors of much more widespread curriculum revisions that will work their way through the schools. Similar revisions are coming in social science, English and foreign language teaching.

- Much greater use will be made of new materials, especially audio-visual materials (including educational TV and closed-circuit TV). Computer-assisted instruction will take hold, though more slowly, partly because of cost, partly because of the difficulty in developing the "software."

- To complement the trend toward individualized learning, there will be more emphasis on counseling (career selection, college selection, emotional problems).

- There will be increased emphasis on, and modernization of, vocational courses, with companies (and unions) participating more in the structuring — and even the conduct — of these courses.

However, despite the potential for improvement in the educational system represented by these and other developments, there will need to be a real struggle to prevent a relative decline in the quality of education. The growing demand for college-level education is likely to result in a diffusion of the supply of competent teachers; and there will be a continuing temptation to lower the degree qualifications in an effort to meet the increasing requirements for graduates. A major question remains, therefore, as to how successful colleges will be in attracting competent teachers and in resisting the temptation to lower their standards.

Perhaps the most significant new education institution to appear on the scene will be the community (or junior) college. These latest additions to the educational system are expected to experience the most rapid expansion in the next ten years. Eventually, there could be one of these two-year colleges in every city of 50,000–100,000 inhabitants, providing an element of higher education for nearly half of our total population.

With education fast becoming a life-long process, it will outgrow the ability of the traditional educational institutions (schools, colleges and universities) to deal with it, regardless of any expansion in their facilities and staff. Education will represent an increasing portion of an individual's time, whatever career he may choose; and, as a consequence, education will become a partnership of business, unions, government, educational and other organizations, and the process beyond the high school-college phase will be far more institutionalized.

Precisely what form that process will take is far from clear, but it will certainly involve a far more permanent on-going relationship between an individual and his education than is the case presently with occasional courses and night classes. Some form of sabbatical leaves system (though not necessarily for a full year) may well be developed, and there will be a growing practice of organizations allowing their professional and technical staff regular time off to pursue their own research, studies and self-development. In short, a broader and more permissive attitude will be taken by organizations toward the educational offerings made available to their employees.

This continuing education/development process will have to be extended from the managerial-professional ranks to other, non-college-education employees. Only in this way will we be able to avoid the pitfall of creating a new version of a "two-class" work force; and only thus will we ensure development of a truly fluid and open society and the full utilization of every individual's abilities.

5

CHANGING VALUE SYSTEMS

One of the more significant findings to emerge from our future environment study has been the evidence of widespread and profound changes in attitudes. Among the many aspects of change that were cited were:

- A generation gap in attitudes toward money;
- Emphasis on the "quality of life";
- The public's lower frustration tolerance;
- Changing attitudes toward work and leisure;
- Education's impact on people's self-image;
- Rejection of authoritarianism and dogmatism;
- Greater emphasis on pluralism and individualism.

To highlight these attitudinal changes is not, of course, to deny the importance of purely physical changes — new technology, more income, new products, better housing, faster transportation. But the fact remains that it is value changes, working slowly and in virtually imperceptible ways, which can cause more profound dislocation in our social organizations. And the changes listed above would, in their combined impact, amount to a values revolution of considerable proportions, affecting virtually every aspect of public and private life.

For business, as for any institution, it therefore becomes vitally important to anticipate and analyze these impending changes. For one thing, if these projections prove to be correct, employees of the future will be differently motivated, have different attitudes toward organization and job structure and live different career patterns. Of equal, if not greater, importance will be the effect of these changing value systems on conditioning the over-all social, political and economic environment in which business will operate. The public's re-written "charter of expectations" of companies (p. 77) would be but one symptom of such a changing climate.

VALUES AND THE STUDENT REVOLTS

The significance, and most probably the pace, of prospective changes in value systems will be heightened by the sheer numbers of the youthful generation. As noted earlier, by 1980 the 20–34 age group will number 58 million, more than one-quarter of the total population. Not only will the conditions affecting value changes be most concentrated in this group, but their numbers alone will ensure that their values will be influential in the general social context.

If we look for a moment at some of the recent campus riots in the United States, we can perceive that they represented a coming together of a number of trends already mentioned — the demands for participation (in university government, curriculum design, appointment of faculty); anti-authoritarianism (rejection of administration-imposed dormitory rules); emphasis on individualism (opposition to mass classes, standardized grading and stereotyped courses); rejection of old institutions (the establishment of "free universities"); search for a new "quality of life" (insistence that universities disassociate themselves from "racist policies" and the "military-industrial complex").

92

It is significant that these forces have impacted first, and most violently, on our universities. Education and affluence are the primary causes of these forces, and the university population is not only the best-educated segment of society but enjoys an above-average level of affluence. Then, too, educational institutions have been traditionally slow to change and innovate in their own structure and procedures. The result has been a growing dissonance between individual aspirations and institutional performance. Not surprisingly, perhaps, universities have been least well prepared to deal with some of the consequences of the higher education they themselves have been developing in their students.

The question for other institutions, and for the future, remains: what will be the impact of this generation of college students on the world of work? So far they have left their mark on society at each stage of their lives:

- As part of the 1946–1949 baby boom, they gave added impetus to the movement to, and growth of, suburbia.

- In the late Fifties and Sixties, they were responsible for an explosive growth in elementary and secondary school construction and for a new emphasis on education in the ordering of state and local priorities.

- As high school students, they have aroused concern for juvenile delinquency, drugs, teen-age crime.

- Now they are crowding into, and revolutionizing, our colleges and universities.

And the process does not seem likely to be interrupted at this point.

It is not so much that radical extremism and violence will be continued directly into the worlds of business, government, unions, non-profit institutions and the like. For one thing, the militant element in the student body is small (estimates vary from 2 to 5 percent) and, after initial successes in catalyzing the support of a larger body for specific causes, seems now to be on the brink of alienating this wider support by their violence and lack of constructive alternatives. Opposition to radical tactics has been developing rapidly among other students, alumni, legislators and even (recently) faculty. The strong probability is that, given any reasonable choice between reform and revolution, the great majority of even today's "concerned" college graduates will choose the former.

But this violence is only an extreme manifestation of the "lower frustration tolerance" discussed earlier. And it is this quality and other value changes of a much larger component of the student body — perhaps 35 to 40 percent — that may set the tone, not only of the work environment, but also of much of the socio-political climate. The impatience and frustration of this larger group is heightened by a feeling of powerlessness in essential matters, a belief that there are forces loose in the world — war, technology, pollution, urban blight, to name a few — that are beyond their, or even society's, control.

Students in the Forties and Fifties grew up in the aftermath of the Depression and World War II — enormous problems, but problems solved, with real "victories" to point to. In the Sixties, continued economic success has been taken for granted, but the new problems have appeared more intractable — Vietnam has been a stalemate; race relations have worsened; our cities appear to them to be virtually un-manageable. The lack of tangible victories so far on these fronts has led to concern, impatience, despair or (in the case of a few) a desire for a radical sweeping away of all existing institutions.

THE MASLOW HIERARCHY

One way of anticipating probable changes in values, attitudes and be-havior is to view them as the consequences of a progression, on a national scale, up Maslow's hierarchy of needs (see box, p. 95). This way of looking at human needs is valuable as a predictor of be-havior and attitudes, because progression tends to be in a single di-rection (upwards, from the first to the fifth levels) rather than random. Since man is a creature of seemingly endless needs, we can predict that, when one has been satisfied, another will appear in its place; when one level of needs has been satisfied, man will proceed to the next level. The levels are progressively _less_ essential in terms of sheer survival and _more_ important in terms of living at one's

Maslow's Hierarchy of Needs

Abraham Maslow, of Brandeis University, has postulated that all men share certain basic needs which can be arranged in a hierarchy of five levels, from the most fundamental physiological needs to the needs of intellectual and spiritual fulfillment. The five levels are:

1. Physiological needs: To survive, man needs food, clothing, shelter, rest. As the imperative requirements for staying alive, these represent the most elemental needs.

2. Safety or security needs: When physiological needs are satisfied, man wants to keep and protect what he has: his need then becomes safeguarding against danger, threat or deprivation. Beyond immediate survival, he starts to look to stabilizing his environment for the future.

3. Social needs: At the next level man wants to be part of something larger than himself: he has social needs for belonging, for sharing and association, for giving and receiving friendship and love.

4. Ego needs: These are the needs that relate to one's self-esteem (needs for self-confidence, independence, achievement, competence, knowledge) and one's reputation (needs for status, recognition, appreciation, deserved respect of one's peers).

5. Self-fulfillment needs: Finally comes the need for growth, self-development, self-actualization. As the capstone of all his other needs, man wants to realize the full range of his individual potential as a human being.

A number of observations should be made about the significance and operation of this hierarchy of needs:

- The hierarchy is arranged in terms of importance to living: it proceeds from the "lowest" level (survival) to the "highest" (self-actualization) — the ranking being in accord with traditional ideas of progress from the purely animal level to the fullest development of human potential.

- At each level <u>needs determine values</u> and patterns of behavior: at the survival level, man values food, clothing, shelter, etc., most highly.

- A satisfied need is <u>not</u> a motivator of behavior; once hunger has been satisfied, it no longer has much motivating force.

- A higher-level need includes, as integral parts, all lower-level needs: ego needs, for instance, operate only when survival, security and social needs continue to be met. If a lower-level need should cease to be met, there will then be a regression to the lower level.

fullest human potential (which seems to be the ultimate level of aspiration).

History seems to validate the Maslow hypothesis, at both the national and the individual level. It is possible, for instance, to plot the position on this hierarchy of each nation according to the level(s) at which the majority of its people live. Thus, virtually all the populations of the underdeveloped nations exist at the survival, or (at best) security, level; while in the United States the majority of the vast middle class operates on the basis of social or ego needs. Similarly, an individual may, if conditions are favorable, progress from purely physiological needs in infancy, through security needs in childhood, toward the satisfaction of social and ego needs in adult life.

When discussing shifts in national values, some gross generalizations and over-simplifications have to be made: yet it should be possible to predict major trends and changes in emphasis. In a society as complex and varied as the United States, the population cannot be slotted at one level only, for there are people operating at all levels. A profile of the population makeup, with its various modes of living, will thus be needed to represent the full range of values: and future changes in this profile will be indicative of shifting value systems.

As a start, it is possible to predict that by 1980 there will be fewer people in the poverty class, and so a reduction of emphasis on survival and safety needs nationally. At the other end of the spectrum, increasing affluence, more education and the changing composition of the labor force will mean a rise in the number of high-income individuals, college graduates, professional and managerial personnel, and so an increase in emphasis on social, ego and self-fulfillment needs.

Focusing on levels 3 and 4, it is possible to note an upward shift within the range in the recent past and to project further movement in the future. The Fifties might well be characterized as a decade of belongingness, conformity and the organization man — a time during which perhaps half the adult population operated, by individual disposition, at level 3. In the Sixties the new emphasis on college education and the growth of professional and technical personnel (note the new phrase "A man is now motivated more by concern for professional advancement than by loyalty to his company") brought increased emphasis on knowledge, competence, professional recognition and status. Forces for the future indicate a growth in the level 4 population to a point where they approximate in numbers those at level 3; and, combined, these two segments would account for perhaps two-thirds of our total adult population.

In fact, the significance of this upward movement is somewhat understated if it is viewed solely in terms of numbers of people at each level. This is so for two reasons:

1. The quality of the needs at each level will be progressively upgraded. To take an obvious example, what we now consider adequate for survival and security is at a higher level than in an underdeveloped country or even than it was in this country thirty years ago. We must expect that the poverty-level budget will continue to be raised in accordance with rising expectations of the poor and the public's concept of social justice. Similarly, ego needs can be met by conspicuous consumption or by professional acclaim. There is a clear qualitative difference between these two modes of satisfaction, and the evidence suggests that movement will tend to be away from the former and toward the latter.

2. The trend setters, "influentials" and power-holders of society tend to be heavily concentrated in levels 3, 4, and 5, rather than proportionately distributed throughout the population. Therefore, the influence of these groups in setting the tone and direction of our society is considerably greater than mere numbers alone might suggest.

A POSSIBLE PROFILE OF VALUE CHANGES

Combining, then, the evidence of impending trends with the deductions that can be drawn from the Maslow thesis, it is possible to construct a profile of some of the more significant value changes that will have occurred, or be under way, by 1980. An attempt has been made to present this profile in graphic form in the chart on p. 105. This chart should be viewed not as a detailed scientific measurement, but merely as a useful way of looking at the future. It contains plottings that are meant to be indicative — pointing the way to a more comprehensive and systematic study of value changes — rather than definitive.

To point up the possible attitudinal changes as dramatically as possible, the chart:

- Has been made up of contrasting pairs of values (to a greater or less extent, that is, enhancement of one value implies a diminution of the other — e.g., war versus peace; conformity versus pluralism). Each society and generation has tended to seek its own new balance between these contrasting pairs, with the weight shifting from one side to the other as conditions and attitudes change;
- Emphasizes the value changes likely to be most prevalent among the trend-setting segment of the population (young, well educated, relatively affluent, "committed").

On the chart are plotted two value profiles — one representing the approximate balance struck by today's trend-setters between each pair of values; the other indicating the hypothetical balance that might be struck in 1980. It is important to stress that the chart attempts to predict only values, not events; even though trend-setters may value, say, arms control agreements, events may lag behind their influence (e.g., due to political thinking of the electorate as a whole) or lie outside their control (e.g., regional wars among developing nations).

Although references to these indicated shifts have been made in earlier chapters, it may be helpful to give the basis for the various plottings in some brief accompanying notes:

War (military might)/Peace (economic development)

The ability of the superpowers to exercise their full military might is progressively diminishing; and the basis for international power and influence is beoming economic strength. These changing facts of the international power structure, combined with the developing reaction to the Vietnam war, are likely to produce an appreciable shift in values in favor of, for example, arms control agreements, enlargement of world trade (including, selectively, with countries in the Communist camp).

Nationalism/Internationalism

Though the potency of nationalistic thought cannot now be doubted, several factors will be working to increase the extent to which people are prepared, and find it necessary, to think in international terms. Foremost in these facts, of course, is the growing amount of interdependence among political and economic institutions. The development of the multi-national corporation; easier, cheaper and faster travel; a broadening scope of education; world-wide electronic communications systems — all these are additional factors working in the same direction.

Federal Government/State and Local Government

The mere fact that state and local government expenditures are growing more rapidly than the Federal budget would be enough to suggest that there might be an impending change in the "let Washington do it" attitude. Disillusionment with the Federal government's record in handling social problems, coupled with a growing insistence on participation and on "returning government to the people," tend to accentuate this change. A revitalization of, and a growing belief in, regional, state and community institutions of government will be mutually reinforcing developments.

Public Enterprise/Private Enterprise

Despite the disruptions of the Depression years, public belief in private enterprise as a producer of material goods, particularly consumer goods, has continued at a high level. While a partial reaction to materialism (see below) and a growing concern about "quality" (both in goods and in less tangible ways) might indicate that this evaluation will be called into question, the developing business role in tackling social problems at least offers the possibility of being an offsetting factor. There is likely to be some public ambivalence about this new role for business — wanting it to develop, to make up for governmental failures; yet, initially, at least, suspicious of business' motives in this area. On balance, however, an increased regard for private enterprise is a distinct possibility.

Organization/Individual

As stated on p. 52, organizations "will be operated less and less by the dictates of administrative convenience, more and more to meet the wants and aspirations of their membership." In all types of organization, the rights and position of the individual, due process and participative forms of management will become the dominant mode. It is not too much to say that, for many key employees, an organization will be accepted or rejected according to whether it assists or hinders them in their plans for self-actualization.

Uniformity (conformity)/Pluralism

A concomitant to the growing emphasis on individualism will be the trend away from uniformity and conformity and toward pluralism and diversity. The speed, scope and diversity of change in our society will also demand variety and flexibility (rather than a monolithic response) for its successful management. Not only will there be a greater diversity of small organizations, particularly in the burgeoning non-profit sector, but there will also be greater diversity within larger organizations.

Independence/Interdependence/Sociability/Privacy

As regards relationships among individuals and institutions, it is quite possible that two opposite trends may develop. At the institutional level, the emphasis seems likely to be on interdependence and co-operation. The blurring of the dividing line between public and private sectors; new government-business partnerships; the obsolescence of political and economic boundaries; the growth of an interdisciplinary approach in education; the prevalence of international co-operative arrangements (whether in arms control, space programs or regional economic groupings) — all these are indicators of a growing belief in the values of inclusiveness, cooperation and systems approach over exclusiveness, insularity and compartmentalization. Similarly, at the individual level, specialization and organization structure will stress the team/task force approach and interpersonal relationships.

At the purely personal level, however, privacy will take on new value in a mass society, and the preference will be for a few deep friendships rather than a general sociability (the mark of the need for belongingness). At level 3 of Maslow's hierarchy, the other-directed man is most characteristic; at levels 4 and 5, inner-direction becomes more the mode of living.

Materialism/Quality of Life

As increasing affluence brings possession of material goods more easily within reach, and education induces a greater regard for self-development, materialism progressively loses much of its appeal as a prime motivating force. For those affected most by these twin factors, the search for a new sense of meaning and purpose in life will become a matter of real importance. Although it may be expected that the current student emphasis on the "quality of life" will be somewhat muted by more material concerns as they move into the world of work, the trend to a new concern for quality and the human dimension in a technological world is most likely to continue.

Status quo (permanence, routine)/Change (flexibility, innovation)

It is not that value will be placed on "change for the sake of change" (indeed, the probability is that there will be a more discriminating attitude as to what change is desirable in its <u>total</u> impact), but unquestionably the balance will be tipped away from preservation of the status quo. Already the forces of technology and education are making themselves felt by compelling recognition of the need for continuous innovation and flexibility (both in institutions and in individuals). The evidence is that the momentum of these forces will increase over the next decade.

Future/Immediacy

One of the more significant characteristics of the "now" generation is the greater value that is being placed on immediate gratification. As noted above, change undermines value in the status quo (the past). It also makes planning for the future difficult and uncertain: indeed, the record of the Sixties has robbed some of hope for the future, and impatience with problems leads many to demand instant solutions. To cite one specific, it may well be that we shall see an undermining of the traditional virtue of "saving for a rainy day," especially if (as expected) public and private programs work more and more toward the goal of income maintenance.

Work/Leisure

The prospective shifts in balance between these two values were discussed in detail on pp. 41–44.

Authority/Participation

The democratizing effect of technology and the rising level of education combine to change the nature of authority and limit its arbitrary exercise. The scope and impact of authority may well be increased,*

---

*Certainly this will be true in absolute terms, as scale and interdependence of organizations increase.

but increasingly it will be the authority of knowledge rather than the authority of position alone. And, since those in authority will be dependent for much of this knowledge on the expertise of specialist professionals, the processes of decision-making will necessarily tend toward a more participative mode.

Centralization/Decentralization

There has been a clear over-all trend toward centralization over at least the past thirty years, both in government and in some aspects of business. It is arguable that this trend may be continued as, for instance, national problems demand national solutions. However, the arguments have already been noted (pp. 63–65) for a changing role at the Federal level and for a considerable decentralization of operational programs to the local level. In the business field, some projections of centralization are made on the basis of the computer's ability to assemble and analyze data gathered from many locations. Unquestionably, this is (or will be) technically feasible, but it would run counter both to business needs for flexibility and decentralized response to change and to demands for responsibility and participation on the part of younger managers and professionals. Further, centrally collected and analyzed data can be made available, by time-sharing processes, to managers in decentralized components to improve their performance.

Ideology (dogma)/Pragmatism (rationality)

However the current debate on the "death of ideology" is resolved, it should not be interpreted as implying an end to the power of ideas. Indeed, the original report noted the greater importance that will be attached to ideas in the form of innovative, theoretical knowledge. However, the notion of imposed dogma, uncritically accepted, will be progressively undermined by a growing conviction that only ideas that can stand the test of individual intellectual examination are worth holding. There will also be a greater willingness to test new ideas, and to accept those that work, without regard to "ideological purity."

Moral Absolutes/Situation Ethics*

In ethical as in intellectual matters, the trend will be toward internalized rather than externalized standards. To an increasing extent, each person will construct his own private value system; and religious institutions will be "used" by their members to aid them in the articulation of their subjective beliefs, not as sources of objective moral truth. However, the concept of moral absolutes is so deeply engrained in our culture that the divergence from the historical norm is not likely to be great in the population as a whole.

Economic Efficiency/"Social Justice"

Economic efficiency is a prime value in a society that is primarily concerned with the production and distribution of material goods. Although individuals benefit from the resulting material wealth, efficiency is rated as an organizational value. As more and more individuals progress beyond the material concerns on Maslow's hierarchy, and so organizational values are diminished in favor of individual values, the ranking of efficiency in the scale of values will tend to be reduced — to nearer a parity with social values such as justice, equality, individual dignity.

On the other hand, social action programs such as education, manpower development programs and urban renewal will be expected to meet higher standards of over-all social efficiency, as measured by a social accounting system.

Means/Ends

Parallel with the concern for efficiency has been a concentration on devising the means (particularly, the technological means) to satisfy immediate needs. There is evidence now of a growing concern that technology has taken on such momentum that it is in danger of dictating, rather than serving, social goals. The new emphasis on the

---

*"Situation ethics" refers to a developing theory that moral decisions should not be based exclusively on absolute imperatives, but shaped, in part, by the particular situation in which they are made.

"quality of life" and the "human dimension" suggests that in the future, means will be subordinated to ends (goals) — which means that greater attention will be devoted to spelling out national and institutional goals.

PROFILE OF SIGNIFICANT VALUE—SYSTEM CHANGES: 1969 - 1980

1969 | 1980

War (military might)		Peace (economic development)
Nationalism		Inter-nationalism
Federal government		State/local government
Public enterprise		Private enterprise
Organization		Individual
Uniformity/conformity		Pluralism
Independence		Interdependence
Sociability		Privacy
Materialism		Quality of life
Status quo/permanence/routine		Change/flexibility/innovation
Future planning		Immediacy
Work		Leisure
Authority		Participation
Centralization		Decentralization
Ideology/dogma		Pragmatism/rationality
Moral absolutes		Situation ethics
Economic efficiency		"Social justice"
Means (esp. technology)		Ends (goals)

——————— 1969 Values Profile

— — — — — 1980 Values Profile

105

6

SOME RELATED QUESTIONS

Any perceptive reader of these chapters must find himself raising
questions about, or taking issue with, specific projections. These
are questions that can be resolved, to an individual's satisfaction,
only by further research and analysis. A basic purpose of this volume is _not_ to engineer an uncritical acceptance of this particular set
of forecasts, but rather to catalyze the broadest possible investigation of future trends and their implications for business planning.
By linking up these independent research points through exchange of
ideas and information, business might be able to build up an effective
"early warning system" of interlocking environmental "radar
stations."

There are, however, a number of broad questions of such general
relevance that it is worth considering them in this context. The
questions most generally asked can be grouped under three major
headings:

1. The question of <u>complacency</u> — does the study take too complacent a view of the future and understate the amount of revolutionary change that is likely to occur?

2. The question of <u>inevitability</u> — are all the predicted developments inevitable (and equally so), or are there varying degrees of probability attached to them?

3. The question of <u>desirability</u> — how desirable are these predicted changes in our society?

1. THE QUESTION OF COMPLACENCY

Some may consider that the study is unduly optimistic and complacent in predicting what might be considered a glowing future for the individual and an unrealistic degree of stability for our institutions. On the first point, it might be possible to cite the predictions of individual affluence, rising education, less arduous work, increased leisure, heightened respect for individual dignity, reduced economic insecurity. As for institutions, these observers might argue that there is insufficient attention to what they see as imminent radical changes in the structure and orientation of our society.

The first thing that needs to be said is that the coming decade (and perhaps any period in an era of radical change) will be characterized by tensions, uncertainty and temporariness. Individual evidences of this are scattered through the report, but there is perhaps a need to bring these points together to underscore this salient characteristic of the Seventies. Certainly, it would.be completely unrealistic to try to maintain an air of complacency in the face of:

- The difficulty of managing a multi-polar world;
- Prolonged uncertainty of local or regional tension and conflict in the world;
- The population explosion;
- Problems of economic development;
- "North-South" polarization;
- The certainty of racial troubles in the United States and the danger of a polarization of American society;
- The related problems of urban decay and environmental pollution;
- The public's "lower frustration tolerance";
- The "generation gap";

- Problems of inflation and intensified foreign competition;
- The drive for greater participation in the decision-making processes of politics, education, business and unions;
- The "research and development explosion" with its constant obsoleting of products, processes, materials and skills;
- The near-revolutionary reform of education.

Even this partial listing should be sufficient to point up the "uncomfortableness" (at the very least) of the next decade. For individuals, there will be a testing of just how much flux the human constitution can endure: for institutions, there remains the question of their capacity to change fast enough to ensure growth or even survival.

Whether all this constitutes a "revolutionary" or an "evolutionary" process is perhaps a matter of individual preference in semantics. Having discounted the probability of radicalization of society (in the political sense), we are nevertheless confronted with a catalogue of changes that, in total, amount to a profound reshaping of individual life-styles and institutional organization and processes.

Again, whether one is optimistic or pessimistic as to how well these problems and uncertainties will be managed depends upon one's view of the effectiveness and speed of countervailing forces. To say that these forces will probably succeed is not to deny the possibility that they might fail. In many instances — most notably in racial and urban problems — there is a delicate balance between success and failure. At this time, a majority of informed opinion still seems inclined to take an optimistic, though certainly not a complacent, view of future trends; but one must always admit the possibility of failure.

Of particular concern to businessmen must be the danger of mistaking the impact of social trends on their own organizations. Since there is a deep-seated tendency in most individuals and organizations to under-estimate the extent to which they will be called upon to change, businessmen must strive for the greatest possible objectivity in this regard. Their general expectancy should be that business, which inevitably is affected by so many social, political and economic forces, will be subject to at least as much organizational change as any institution in our society.

Three points should be made in this connection:

(a) The detailed analysis of the implications of societal change for business has not yet been undertaken in this study. Some possibilities have begun to be explored; but to stop at this preliminary stage of analysis would be to maximize the possibility of under-estimating needed changes in the organization.

(b) Many indicators of probable business response to change are already visible in sporadic and undeveloped form — hence the use of terms such as "more" flexibility and "less" rigidity. However, the full development of all (or most) of these responses in a single company would represent a change of major proportions over the course of a decade.

(c) Once again, merely bringing together in one list all of the possible structural changes mentioned in the report would dramatize the total impact in a way that scattered references cannot fully do, e.g.:

- The use of temporary task forces and project teams;
- The possibility of modular work scheduling;
- Re-structuring of work assignments;
- New styles of organization and managing;
- Re-structuring around a research or services focus (rather than a manufacturing focus);
- New partnerships with government;
- New partnerships with education.

Perhaps of even greater significance to business will be the challenge, hinted at in previous passages, to some of its basic values — work, efficiency, profit, growth, technology, organizational goals. To some extent, each one of these basic business values will be subject to questioning, erosion and attack. Developed over another ten years, these forces could fundamentally re-shape the goals, thinking and operations of many businesses.

However, it remains true, for any organization, that it will have to guard against the pitfall of believing that it alone will be called upon to change less than others in adapting to new conditions. A contrary pitfall is, of course, the assumption that nothing can be done to shape change, that we are all in the grip of blind, impersonal forces and that successful and timely reaction is the most we can hope for.

2. THE QUESTION OF INEVITABILITY

It is perhaps unavoidable, in a study of this nature, to give the impression that the events and trends discussed in it will occur. However, it is vital, at the outset, to dispel this notion of inevitability: otherwise the limits of possible corporate or individual action will be drawn too restrictively.

In the first place, none of the trends or events can be, at this distance in time, quite literally "inevitable." If they were, then there should be complete certainty and agreement on the prediction; and this is certainly not the case. However strong a consensus there may be about a given prediction, it is clearly based upon a multitude of explicit or implicit assumptions such as:

(a) Assumption of no nuclear holocaust — most experts state that a nuclear war is most unlikely to occur: but if this assumption proves wrong, clearly "all bets are off."

(b) Assumption of supportive action — for the prediction of economic stabilization to be realized, for instance, it is necessary to assume that the sort of actions by business and government spelled out in this study will, in fact, be taken. Stabilization, in other words, is not so inevitable that it will "just happen," regardless of the action or inaction of a multitude of individuals or organizations.

In predicting developments over a decade, it is far more meaningful to talk in terms of degrees of relative probability. In the final analysis assigning probability to a trend or future event is essentially a matter of judgment, after weighing the known data and cross-checking with informed opinion. A further cross-check can be run by plotting the predictions along a probability axis so that their relative positions are made apparent.

It is also helpful to assess the probable "diffusion" of a trend or event — that is, the extent to which it is likely to be uniformly distributed over the population to which it applies (world, U.S.A., an industry, etc.) or relatively confined to a segment of that population. Again, plotting the predictions along a diffusion axis makes explicit, in a coordinated fashion, the relative weightings assigned in separate judgments.

111

Combining these axes into a probability/diffusion matrix, as is done on the chart on p. 113, serves as a check on the internal consistency of a relatively large number of predictions, from two viewpoints. By itself, such a matrix adds little to a scientific approach to environmental forecasting, but it does provide a way of looking at the future that may perhaps be helpful.

The plottings made in this matrix are largely for purposes of illustration and not to be taken as final judgments. To the extent that they provoke debate, they will at least demonstrate the value of making judgments clearly explicit so that planned action can more surely be taken. A few words of explanation about a sampling of the plottings may help to make clear the basis for them:

(a) The probability of thermonuclear war is generally judged to be low; but if it did occur, its catastrophic impact would be felt world-wide. Hence it is assigned a low probability/high diffusion rating.

(b) Regional or local wars in the developing nations, on the other hand, are much more likely to occur, but they will be confined to relatively limited areas. Consequently, they are assigned a high probability/low diffusion rating.

(c) At the high end of the probability axis, there are three developments with different plottings on the diffusion axis:

   i. Levels of education should rise, in absolute terms, for virtually all segments of the U.S. population;

   ii. Unemployment rates should remain generally low, but the averages will cover a diversity of rates for various skill, age and racial groups.

   iii. Even more is diversity true of per capita disposable income which, while increasing an average of 50 percent in fifteen years, will do so at different rates for different groups, possibly even increasing the gap between the "new affluents" and the smaller, but more visible, poverty class.

(d) Some form of new income-maintenance program will most probably be in force within the next three years or so; the questions at this time are (i) whether it will be a system of cash allowance that would affect most of the population or a more selective program such as a negative income tax and (ii) how an incentive to employment will be built into the system.

Whatever the limitations inherent in such an approach may be, it does have the merit of handling future trends on something other than a basis of flat inevitability.

3.   THE QUESTION OF DESIRABILITY

Even among those interviewed in the course of this study, the desirability of the predictions they were discussing was questioned by some. As we noted in the opening chapter (p. 12), "differing attitudes to the trends were manifest, and differing policy implications might be drawn, but there was general agreement on the basic facts of the developing trends." It goes without saying, therefore, that reaction to the projections will range from delight to despair. To some it may seem as if the millennium is being foreshadowed; to others, the decadent end of enduring societal values. Our study has attempted to present these forecasts, however, without making judgments as to their desirability.

Probability/Diffusion* Matrix
for Events and Trends Occurring by 1980 (Based on assessments made in July, 1969)

Low				PROBABILITY				High		
Thermo-nuclear war					3% inflation		Federal funding of welfare			High
		Increased price of gold		Flexible exchange rates	35-hr. work week				Rising level of education	
							↗ ?			
						Income mainte-nance				DIFFUSION*
							↘ ?	3-4.5% unemployment		
	Detroit-type riots			Retirement at 55						
		Strikes outlawed						$3,600 per capita income		
						Regional wars				Low

*"Diffusion" represents the extent to which a trend or development will be uniformly distributed over the population to which it applies.

113

Such judgments will, nevertheless, inevitably be made — and indeed should be made, as a necessary prelude to <u>action</u>. As noted above, events do not "just happen": individuals and organizations cause them to happen. And forecasting has a purpose beyond being an interesting intellectual exercise: it is intended to guide imaginative and timely action. Judgments concerning both probability and desirability are, therefore, integral parts of the planning process.

One problem is that subjective judgments of desirability can cloud one's assessment of probability. There is a human bias toward a process of reasoning that goes: "I don't like this forecast: it goes against my grain and my experience, and I cannot really believe it will occur ... ." and then the unspoken, even unrecognized conclusion: "Therefore it won't occur." It thus becomes particularly important to arrive at assessments of probability in a more objective framework, and <u>prior</u> to judgments of desirability.

7

"ACT—NOT RE-ACT"

If we are to be the masters of our fate, rather than the victims of circumstance, there can be no alternative to espousing an activist philosophy in dealing with the external forces that shape our environment. No organization — least of all business — can now be regarded as a self-contained, entirely self-regulating system. All are linked with others in a complex, interdependent economy and society: all are shaped, to a greater or less degree, not only by the broad social, political and economic forces that determine our course as a nation, but also by the actions, or inaction, of other organizations.

As business managers, therefore, we have a choice of letting events run their course and merely responding to their dictates; or of helping shape events, particularly those that will impact most heavily on our businesses. If, however, we select the first option, we must recognize that we thereby condemn our organizations to dancing to a tune chosen by others and that, on many important matters, the real power of decision-making will have been taken from our hands.

If we would rather help shape events, in an effort to exert some measure of control over our destinies, there is one cardinal principle we must adhere to. "Act — not re-act." To attain any degree of success in this venture, two things are required:

1. A commitment to conscious and sustained intervention in the external affairs of one's business environment;

2. Sufficient lead time before the full development of a trend or event for this intervention to be effective.

It is not enough for this external involvement to be random and sporadic: in an environment changing as rapidly and extensively as ours will in the Seventies, this action must be planned and continuous. It must also, obviously, be timely.

It is precisely to help assure this timeliness of action that an environmental forecasting system such as we have discussed is urgently needed in most businesses. Notwithstanding the speed of change, it still requires a lead time of two to five years for any program of business action to start having an appreciable effect on its environment — almost certainly longer if a reversal of current trends is being contemplated. It is a truism to say that one cannot change overnight the quantity and quality of the available work force; the political climate on labor legislation; public attitudes on business' social responsibility or the state of racial relations in a community. Such changes require sustained and patient effort, not by business alone, but by many organizations and individuals.

This commitment to action will require of business a greater willingness to work in national and community coalitions. The "limits of the possible" for one company (or even several companies) alone must necessarily be severely restricted, by the size and complexity of the problems to be solved. The trend toward interdependence itself suggests the probability that co-operative action among differing types of organization will become a normal pattern in dealing with social problems. It is for this reason (among others) that business managers will have to develop greater economic and political sophistication and (as we noted earlier) "an instinct for survival in a political world."

An "early warning system," then, can do little more than buy us the needed time for action. It cannot diminish the range of our problems, nor guarantee the wisdom of our choices or the success of our efforts. It can achieve only the more limited objective of increasing the probability that our selection of goals and means will be more deliberate and purposeful. Perhaps it will be seen to have had its major effect if it succeeds in jarring business from a complacent philosophy of response.

Responsiveness to environmental forces is, in itself, an essential and desirable characteristic in any organization. But, alone, it cannot be an adequate course of action for an organization that seeks to maintain its vitality in a fast-changing environment. Only by seizing the initiative can organizational self-renewal be attained. This is particularly true in the case of business which, historically, has built its place in society on its entrepreneurial ability. To retain and enhance its standing in the society of the Seventies, business can do no less than accelerate the vitality and creativity of the initiatives it determines to take.

Appendix A

Interviews Held in Connection with General Electric's Future Environment Study

EDUCATORS

Professor Dean S. Ammer, Director, Bureau of Business and Economic Research, Northeastern University.

Professor Kenneth R. Andrews, Graduate School of Business Administration, Harvard University.

Dean Nathan Baily, School of Business, American University.

Father Raymond C. Baumhart, S.J., former Research Associate, Cambridge Center for Social Studies; Executive Vice President, Loyola University.*

---

*Father Baumhart also arranged a symposium for this discussion at the Cambridge Center. Also present on that occasion were:

Father Leo Brown	Father Donald Wolf
Father Joseph Becker	Father Thomas McMahon
Father John Thomas	Father Peter Henriot
Father William Mehok	Father William Lawlor

Professor John Blum, Professor of History, Yale University.

Professor Wayne G. Broehl, Jr., Amos Tuck School of Business Administration, Dartmouth College.

Professor Yale Brozen, Graduate School of Business, University of Chicago.

Dean Robert G. Cox, School of Business, Syracuse University.

Dr. Joseph Finklestein, Professor of History and Economics; Chairman, Department of History, Union College.

Dr. Bela Gold, Professor of Industrial Economics, Case Western Reserve University.

Professor William Gomberg, Wharton School, University of Pennsylvania.

Dr. Mason Haire, Alfred P. Sloane School of Management, Massachusetts Institute of Technology.

Dr. Oscar Handlin, Director, Charles Warren Center for Studies in American History, Harvard University.

Professor M. Thomas Kennedy, Graduate School of Business Administration, Harvard University.

Dr. Sar Levitan, George Washington University.

Professor Robert M. MacDonald, Amos Tuck School of Business Administration, Dartmouth College.

Professor Raymond W. Mack, Director, Center for Urban Affairs, Northwestern University.

Dr. Emmanuel G. Mesthene, Executive Director, Harvard University Program on Technology and Society.

Dean William Moekel, School of Business, Miami University.

Dean David G. Moore, New York State School of Industrial and Labor Relations, Cornell University.*

Dr. Wilbert E. Moore, Russell Sage Foundation.

---

*Dean Moore also arranged for a colloquium at which the following were present:

Professor Walter Galenson	Professor Wayne Hodges
Professor George Hildebrand	Professor Frank Miller
Professor John Hinrichs	Professor Maurice Neufield

Professor Wallace S. Sayre, Department of Public Law and Government, Columbia University.

Dr. George P. Shultz, formerly Dean, Graduate School of Business, University of Chicago; Secretary of Labor.

Dr. George W. Taylor, Wharton School, University of Pennsylvania.

Professor Melvin M. Tumin, Professor of Sociology and Anthropology, Princeton University.

Professor Robert C. Turner, Professor of Business Economics and Public Policy, Graduate School of Business, Indiana University.

Professor Victor H. Vroom, Graduate School of Industrial Administration, Carnegie-Mellon University.

Dr. Allen Wallis, President, University of Rochester.

Dr. Clarence C. Walton, formerly Dean, School of General Studies, Columbia University; President, Catholic University.

Dr. Stanton Wheeler, Russell Sage Foundation.

Professor Donald J. White, Associate Professor of Economics, Boston College.

Dean Robert R. White, School of Management, Case Western Reserve University.

Dr. Henry M. Wriston, former Chairman of President Eisenhower's Commission on National Goals; former president, Brown University.

GOVERNMENT, PRESS AND
ASSOCIATION REPRESENTATIVES

Representative Leslie C. Arends, Illinois.

Stanley H. Brams, Publisher and Editor, Detroit Labor Trends.

Dr. Eugene S. Callender, President, New York Urban Coalition.

Thomas Curtis, former Representative, Missouri.

Ralph de Toledano, author and columnist, King Features Syndicate.

Representative Charles Diggs, Michigan.

Edward H. Donnel, Jr., executive editor, Bureau of National Affairs.

Senator Paul J. Fannin, Arizona.

Representative Paul Findley, Illinois.

George Hagedorn, Director of Economic Studies, National Association of Manufacturers.

Senator Clifford P. Hansen, Wyoming.

Herman Kahn, Director, Hudson Institute.

Glenard P. Lipscomb, Late Representative, California.

Dr. James McBride, The Center for Strategic Studies.

Senator Gale W. McGee, Wyoming.

Raymond J. McHugh, General Manager, Copley News Service.

Thomas Morton, Berkshire Eagle, Pittsfield, Massachusetts.

Senator Claiborne Pell, Rhode Island.

A. H. Raskin, Assistant Editor, Editorial Page, New York Times.

Victor Riesel, syndicated columnist, Hall Syndicate.

Donald Robinson, National Association of Manufacturers.

Dr. Emerson P. Schmidt, Economic Consultant, Chamber of Commerce of the United States.

Albert T. Sommers, Vice President and Director, Divison of Economic Research, National Industrial Conference Board.

Representative William A. Steiger, Wisconsin.

Edward T. Townsend, Labor Editor, Business Week.

Norman Walker, Federal Mediation and Conciliation Service.

Mrs. Alice Widener, Syndicated columnist and publisher of USA.

Laurence I. Wood, Vice President, Washington Relations, General Electric Company.

Appendix B

Literature Surveyed in Connection with General Electric's Future Environment Study

Books

Bennis, Warren G., and Philip E. Slater, The Temporary Society, Harper & Row, 1968.

Brookings Institution, Agenda for the Nation, Brookings Institution, 1968.

Chase, Stuart, The Most Probable World, Harper & Row, 1968.

William R. Ewald, Editor, Environment and Change: The Next Fifty Years, papers for the American Institute of Planners' 50 Year Consultation, Indiana University Press, 1968.

Foreign Policy Association, Toward the Year 2018, Cowles Education Corp., 1968.

Galbraith, John K., The New Industrial State, Houghton Mifflin Company, 1967.

Hacker, Andrew, Editor, The Corporation Take-Over, Harper & Row, 1964.

- Chap. 9, "Caught on the Horn of Plenty" - W. H. Ferry
- Chap. 10, "Cybernation: The Silent Conquest" - D. N. Michael
- Chap. 11, "Decline of the Labor Movement" - S. Barkin
- Chap. 12, "Politics and the Corporation" - A. Hacker

Kahn, Herman, and Anthony J. Wiener, The Year 2000: A Framework for Speculation on the Next Thirty-three Years, Macmillan, 1967.

Mack, Raymond W., Transforming America, Random House, 1967.

Michael, Donald N., The Next Generation, Vintage Books, 1965.

Tyler, Gus, The Labor Revolution, Viking Press, 1966.

Young, Whitney Jr., Beyond Racism, McGraw-Hill, 1969.

National Commission on Technology, Automation and Economic Progress, Technology and the American Economy, Government Printing Office, February, 1966.

Conference Papers

American Academy of Arts and Sciences and Amos Tuck School of Business Administration, Dartmouth College, Conference on Business and Society (September 29–30, 1966).

American Assembly, Challenges to Collective Bargaining (October 27–30, 1966).

Papers by Arnold Weber, Jack Stieber, A. H. Raskin, John Dunlop, Ray Marshall, Benjamin Aaron and Melvin Rothbaum

Labor Management Institute of the American Arbitration Association, Adaptation of Collective Bargaining to Our Changing Environment (November 20–23, 1966).

Papers by:

Neil Chamberlain
H. Northrup, Margaret Chandler and W. Gomberg
Robert McKersie
J. Dunlop and M. W. Reder

U. S. Chamber of Commerce, Forum for Economic and Political Discussion (Airlie House, Warrenton, Va., June 4-9, 1967): papers and supplementary readings:

Papers by:	Supplementary Reading from:
John Dunlop	Sumner Slichter
Henry Wallich	John Kenneth Galbraith Leonard A. Lecht
Wilbert E. Moore	Daniel Bell
Henry W. Malcolm	Marshall McLuhan Paul Goodman
Norton E. Long	Theodore Draper Paul Goodman Oscar Goss
Peter F. Drucker	Stephen K. Baily
John J. Corson	Robert L. Heilbroner Paul A. Samuelson Edward S. Mason
Marion Folsom	Committee for Economic Development statement on Raising Low Incomes Through Improved Education
Jackie Robinson	
Lloyd V. Berkner	Edwin H. Land Barbara Ward Hans Linsser
Seymour Melman	

Eight State Project on Designing Education for the Future, Prospective Changes in Society by 1980 (First Area Conference: Denver, Colo., July, 1966).

Articles, Speeches, etc.

"The Road to 1977," an article by Max Ways (Fortune, January, 1967).

"Notes on the Post-Industrial Society," two articles by Daniel Bell, The Public Interest, Winter and Spring, 1967 issues.

"Our Changing Environment," a talk by Prof. Kenneth E. Boulding, University of Michigan, to General Electric's General Management Course, Crotonville, N.Y. (October 5, 1965).

"Forecasting Future Public Problems," articles by Olaf Helmer and Theodore Gordon (The Conference Board Record, National Industrial Conference Board, June, 1967).

"New Concepts in Collective Bargaining," address by I. W. Abel to Institute of Industrial Relations, University of California (May 17, 1966).

"The Union Member: Profile and Attitudes," article by Alexander Barkan (AFL-CIO American Federationist, August, 1967).

"Shape of the Future" (a series of articles in The Wall Street Journal, December, 1966 – January, 1967).

"Coalition Bargaining and the Future of Union Structure," article by Herbert J. Lahne (Labor Law Journal, June, 1967).

"The Sources for Future Growth and Decline in American Trade Unions," by Joel Seidman (from the Proceedings of the Seventeenth Annual Meeting, Industrial Relations Research Association).

"Labor's Next Decade" (article in Nation's Business, July, 1965).

"Entering the New Economy" article by Dean S. Ammer (Harvard Business Review, September – October, 1967).

Issues of The Futurist, a publication of the World Future Society.

Appendix C

Trends in Compensation and Benefits

1. *Disappearance of Wage-Salary Difference*

   The growth of benefit programs (especially income security programs and short workweek provisions) over the past twenty years has laid some groundwork for a shift to salary status for the hourly paid workers, and for a gradual transition to annual earnings guarantees for regular workers in some industries.

   Labor market conditions may make guarantees of "salaried-status" virtually a necessity to attract and hold skilled workers; and the cost of substituting salaries for hourly wages — in a "full employment" economy with few layoffs — may be negligible.

2. *Income Maintenance*

   Programs to raise and maintain the income level of employed workers who are above the poverty level will be paralleled by new proposals in public policy to build income maintenance into the system for those in the poverty class (whether employed or not). Various proposals for "minimum income allowance" or a "negative income tax" have been advanced, and there is widespread expectation that _some_ form of income maintenance, on a universal basis, will be enacted within the next three years.

The basic problem to be resolved in designing such a program will, of course, be how to balance concern for dignified living against the need to preserve incentive. The most predicted resolution of this problem will be use of a schedule which reduces allowances partially for an increase in earned income, as opposed to current welfare practice of deducting from cash payments 100 percent of any income earned.

3. _Trend Away from "Piecework"_

A general trend is expected _against_ compensation plans that stress individual output, and _to_ those that focus the attention of the whole organization on all aspects of economic achievement. New technology, which often removes control of output from the individual worker, challenges the validity of output incentives; and the growing importance of the indirect segment of the work force further restricts the applicability of such compensation plans.

Managerial philosophy is changing in the direction of eliminating cleavages within the organization (the trend toward "all salaried" work force also stems, in part, from this philosophy) and is becoming aware that the elimination of "disincentives" is as important as the construction of new incentives.

In the design of compensation plans that take note of these developments — _and_ seek to restrain the wage-salary push — profit sharing may take on added attraction. Professor Neil Chamberlain has stated the case thus:

> If our social aim is price stability, and if we seek to hold wage increases to something in the vicinity of the national average increase in productivity, and if we are realistic enough to expect that the most we can expect from business on the price front is no price

increases, but not actual price decreases, then we have a sure-fire recipe for above-average profits in those companies where there has been above-average productivity improvement. We can scarcely expect a successful hold-the-line policy on wages in such instances, and some form of profit share or investment share or savings share may make good sense.*

4. *Miscellaneous*

  (a) Double time for <u>overtime</u> could become more popular (not to share the work, so much as to pay the needed premium in the new work environment).

  (b) As higher income taxes start to affect the take-home pay of even production workers, they may show interest in <u>deferred compensation</u> plans.

  (c) <u>Vacations</u> will get longer and may be paid at <u>premium</u> rates (to take care of employees' extra expenses).

  (d) There is not expected to be a trend to substantially <u>earlier retirement</u>, though (i) the norm may go down to 62, as in present early retirement plans; and (ii) in some occupations such as trucking, airlines and police, job requirements might dictate a retirement age of, say, 55. (The trend of the early Sixties toward early retirement is seen as an aberration, caused by unwarranted concern over automation.)

  (e) <u>Pensions</u> may be increased to a point at which, together with OASI benefits, they will approach 80–90 percent of latest career earnings. Further moves will be made to legislate funding requirements for pension funds, and there is ex-pected to be an increase in "portability" through earlier vesting rights.

---

  *"Economic, Manpower, Wage-Price Trends and Their Implications," keynote address to the American Management Association's Annual Personnel Conference, February 6–8, 1967.